Pieces of the Plains

Memories and Predictions from the Heart of America

John Janovy, Jr.

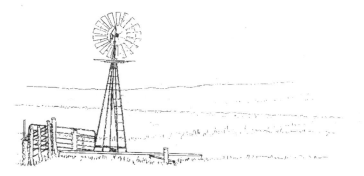

BOOKS BY JOHN JANOVY, JR.
Keith County Journal
Back in Keith County
Yellowlegs
Fields of Friendly Strife
On Becoming a Biologist
Vermilion Sea
Dunwoody Pond
Comes the Millennium
Ten Minute Ecologist
Teaching in Eden
Foundations of Parasitology (with L. S. Roberts)
Outwitting College Professors
The Ginkgo
Pieces of the Plains

http://bsweb.unl.edu/labs/janovy
http://talkparasites.blogspot.com

Sponsored by James and Rhonda Seacrest

Cover photo and drawings by John Janovy, Jr.
Book design by Sheri Ericksen
Publishing services by Lee Booksellers / J & L Lee Co.

ISBN 0-934904-62-6, 978-0-934904-62-9
Printed in the U.S.A.

J&LLeeCo.

Contents

Foreword v

PART I—*Oklahoma*
   1 Ethel   3
   2 Genevieve 19
   3 Red Dirt 35

PART II—*Aksarben Spelled Backward*
   4 Through a Lens 57
        Introduction to "The Horse" 77
   5 The Horse 81
   6 The Firm 93

PART III—*A Future*
   7 What is Science? 119
   8 Why are Politicians so Scientifically Illiterate? 133
   9 What is a Human Being? 151
  10 What Will Human Life Be Like in a
        Couple of Thousand Years? 165

Acknowledgments, Notes, and Sources 181

Foreword

Jim Seacrest sat across from me in a booth at one of our favorite local restaurants, doing exactly what I would have liked to be doing, and would have been doing had I not needed to be at work later that afternoon, namely, studying his Stolichnaya martini on the rocks. As he pulled out the olives, impaled on their little blue plastic sword, he reminded me of something I knew very well:

"I'm a bibliophile," he said trying the martini; it passed inspection. Then he offered to publish this book, the one you are now holding. "Jim McKee and I are venturing back into the business. Here's a copy of our first one." He handed me a trade paperback, one that I knew about because of a presentation by its author, the noted and respected local Congregational minister, Otis Young, who had recently retired. Otis had taken Jim up on an offer to publish any book that he would write and as a result I now held printed versions of the many sermons I'd watched Otis deliver on television. I opened the cover and checked the copyright page; "Sponsored by Jim and Rhonda Seacrest" appeared right above the ISBN. Rhonda and Jim are Nebraskans with exceedingly deep roots in the western prairies, equally deep perspective on the arts and humanities, and even deeper generosity toward the University of Nebraska–Lincoln (UNL), an institution whose health they deem necessary to sustain the intellectual richness they obviously believe is a minimal trait of any civilized society. Their offer to Otis, I'm sure, stemmed from such belief; I perceived their offer to me as pure flattery, no matter what else may have been the motive or rationale.

I do not know why various people write books, but from having written a good many, I suspect such individuals are caught up in a sticky web of arrogance, narcissism, a driving need for self-expression, and at least a little boredom with whatever employment they happen to hold. This web

v

stretches, like some predatory spider's invitation to entrapment, between the branches of opportunity and idealism. I certainly have the idealism, very likely inherited, and carry it proudly, sometimes like a sword, sometimes like a sack of wet garbage, but always as a warning to anyone who, having asked the time of day, could easily end up hearing how to dissect the watch, how to preserve some of its parts, how its wheels and springs can be used to recover its evolutionary history, and why all this information is of vital importance to our nation. Your question—What time is it?—was born of honest ignorance; your answer came from a biology teacher's view of what the world simply must understand about some item's structure, its internal functions, its past, its relatives, and its role in global affairs.

Such idealism probably is what sent me into academia in the first place. As a twenty-something college senior in 1959, suddenly in the company of an ornithologist, I distinctly remember thinking, "I want to be just like this guy." "This guy" was George M. Sutton, Research Professor of Zoology at the University of Oklahoma, and his ongoing conversation with the world concerned structure, function, history, and relationships of birds, of course, but sometimes branched out into art, music, literature, and beauty as well. Sutton often began his classes with a poem; Gerard Manley Hopkins' *The Wind Hover* was the first poetry I ever heard used as a pedagogical device in a biology class. And, Sutton painted pictures of birds, exactly as I had tried to do as a child, using watercolors, although by the time we met he was world renowned for his skill with the medium, having learned at the knee of Louis Agassiz Fuertes, a watercolor purist and perhaps the finest of all bird artists. Here were examples of grown men, responsible citizens, making a life by doing what I'd tried to do for entertainment as a kid. I suspect that contact with ornithologists showed me a person didn't have to grow up, after all. Sutton also wrote books; he was the first person I ever met who had done so.

For the opportunity to be a book writer, indeed the requirement for being one, I must thank the people of Rhonda and Jim Seacrest's beloved state of Nebraska, that is, the taxpayers and parents who have sent their children to UNL. Every single working day, insofar as is physically possible, upon arriving on campus I go straight to the student union, get a grande Estima, or whatever other dark coffee is available at the Starbucks Café Caffina, and a couple of pieces of really dark chocolate, and retire to a favorite table to write for an hour. An hour a day gets you a page a day, which in turn gets you a book a year, and if a third of these books get published, then that's ten or eleven books over a forty-year period.

This creativity hour is available because I am a university professor and on any typical day I've been up since 4:00 A.M. working on class presentations, scientific papers, letters of recommendation, data analysis, and an occasional nasty memo, usually lengthy, to my department chair. Furthermore, after that hour in the union, I'm in my lab, often well into the evening. So although I consider my creativity hour to be well earned, I also recognize that it is a mixture of all those things mentioned above that drive people to write, including the narcissism, as well as the illusion, and sometimes delusion that someone will actually want to read what you've written. Needless to say, when Jim offered to publish anything I'd produce, within seconds I had the opening paragraph in my mind. After a few more seconds, however, our conversation turned to the kind of book this one might become, and Jim had some ideas of his own.

"You could write about Cedar Point," he said, referring to the University of Nebraska's Cedar Point Biological Station (CPBS) where I'd spent the past thirty-three summers teaching and doing research. "You could write about being a biologist, about your students, about the university, about your children, about Karen." He was hinting at what he wanted me to put down on paper for posterity and as a result I mentally rewrote that opening paragraph. I had come to his part of the world forty-three years before our lunch meeting, and his part of the world had provided me with an exceedingly rich life of the mind, an almost constant exposure to the arts, contact with famous people, much recognition for my creative and scholarly efforts, and, eventually, an excellent salary. For forty-three years I had reaped enormous benefits from a place so few Americans ever believed had many, a place called Nebraska. It was now payback time.

If I interpreted our conversation correctly, as well as his intentions in making this publishing offer, Jim wanted me to tell the people of Nebraska just what they had given me, how those gifts had been translated into one individual's Good Life (to borrow a phrase from the state motto), and to tell this personal history in a way that might be useful to future generations. Implicit was the requirement that this history be told in a rather eloquent way, too, in a *book* worthy of inclusion not only in Jim's personal library, but also in personal libraries everywhere there lived a Nebraskan, or former Nebraskan with fond memories of the place, as well as people who might not even know, or care, where Nebraska was to be found but were willing to read a scientist's musings.

As Jim sipped his martini, and I started wishing I'd ordered one, too, the challenge of this freebee publishing offer slowly became obvious. The writer's narcissism was off the table; the writer's burden was on it: do something important, not just something that you believe to be important, and do it in a highly professional, but still original, way. In other words, produce something that will stand the test of time; and, do it within a few months. The offer was not really a freebee; I just considered it so, a case of the writer's arrogance refusing to be completely squashed, a meme-trait that would eventually get squashed because it always does once a project starts and once that blank page (= laptop screen) starts staring at you, asking

"Okay, John; what are you going to do next?"

In the spring of 1966, when I accepted a faculty position at UNL, Karen, my wife of five years at the time, cried; she had in mind Florida or California. When we'd crossed the bridge into town, in August of that year, she'd taken a deep breath through her open car window and declared that Lincoln, Nebraska, smelled just like the New Brunswick, New Jersey, from where we'd come. Forty-three years later, the wife that Jim was suggesting I write about was as deeply rooted as I in this north-central American steppe. Our children grew to adulthood in

Nebraska, then left, at least physically, although our son, John III, the only one born here, eventually returned. Frequently in the evenings, in the Third Millennium's opening years, staring at one another across the kitchen bar over remnants of an old-folks-type meal, Karen and I talk about retirement, about writing one another's obituaries, about local politics, especially academic politics, about all the stuff in our house—most of it of value only because of memories it evokes—and about having become "salt of the earth," a phrase used by my University of Oklahoma doctoral research adviser to describe family friends who'd spent their careers in exactly the same way we'd spent ours: employed by the University of Nebraska. Karen and I also talked, frequently, about leaving.

"So where do you want to move to?" she'd ask. I could never provide a satisfactory answer. If we had this conversation in early February, the places that scrolled through my mind usually were near golf courses several hundred miles south of our kitchen.

"I don't know. Where do you want to move to?" I'd reply. Then I could see her thoughts, see her mentally cataloging the elements of her life: her children, our close personal friends, the smell of our home, the Sheldon Museum of Art where she worked, changing scenery of her drive into town, and most of all her back yard, a living sculpture comprising about one ten-thousandth of a square mile of hosta, day lilies, iris, roses, impatiens, geraniums, and at least a dozen more cultivars, a sculpture needing constant hands-on—but therapeutic—maintenance for eight months every year. We were not moving anywhere, at least on purpose. The roots we'd put down in 1966 had grown too deep, like some big bluestem tussock's metastasizing reticulum that bound together an entire community of relationships, an historical record of metaphorical droughts, floods, and storms, gorgeous spring and quiet Indian Summer days, and late night conversations around our dining room table, all into a near-indestructible union between the Earth and its "salt."

In essence, then, this book is intended to make permanent the American Great Plains experience as lived by one individual whose profession is the study of nature and whose daily life, like those of all other Americans, has been and still is shaped by the global forces at work during the last half of the twentieth century. This book also truly is a freebee in one sense, though, regardless of the challenges involved in producing it. No literary agents, no publishing house editors with dollar signs covering their glasses, and no peer-review scientists, passed judgment on it prior to publication. Rhonda and Jim Seacrest therefore treated me exactly like I've treated hundreds of my students, asking me to solve some problem not by finding an answer, but by making one. So I responded to the assignment in exactly the same way I've wished those hundreds of students each had responded by contributing what I believe to be my very best work. "Best" in this case means most creative, most original, most visionary, most experimental and exploratory, but, of course, grammatically and stylistically correct, although with an acknowledgment that grammar and style often must be subordinate to originality if a writer, or an artist or composer, or even a scientist, is to contribute something new to the human conversation about the world we occupy for such a brief time. But be forewarned: most of my best work has been rejected repeatedly by the commercial world.

Pieces of the Plains is a book mainly about our intellectual and emotional interactions with nature, although "interactions" is defined rather broadly. I am a scientist, a professional biologist who does research and teaches at several levels, from freshmen to doctoral candidates. I also write books, some of which get published. Successful writers eventually learn to follow the dictum "write about what you know," and *Pieces* certainly adheres to that advice. The essays are organized into sections beginning with Part I—Oklahoma, which includes two chapters about Karen's family and her history, and one about my grandfather. Each of these pieces has an "afterword" attached, an explanation of how and where it came about and what my intent was in writing it. Thus I open with backstory.

None of us come into the world with a completely clean slate; we all carry the burden of a time and place where we first see the light of day and first hear the words of those attending our birth, and we have no say whatsoever in the sights, sounds, smells, and touches that we experience for the next year or two. By the time we reach kindergarten, we've been told the stories, read the nursery rhymes, and steeped in whatever traditions our extended family possesses simply by being alive in a particular part of the world, at a particular period of history, and as a member of some culture. By the time we get over our teenage rebellion against loving parents, the time and place of our existence is as permanently embedded in our being as would be some tattoo of the mind. Part I—Oklahoma is about this mental tattoo, and I've tried to write it in a way that makes a reader put the book down for a while in order to review his or her own circumstances of birth and maturity. As a result of reading Part I, I hope you understand how kids end up deciding to study nature for the rest of their lives. You should also know that at my sixth grade graduation ceremony in Oklahoma City, some of my classmates predicted I would be a scientist; this prediction was made in the spring of 1949.

Part II—Aksarben Spelled Backward focuses on the present, which is to say, the last forty-three years of life in Lincoln, Nebraska, and as an employee of UNL. (*Aksarben*, of course, is "Nebraska" spelled backward, a term used in various contexts principally in Omaha.) When you start a family of your own, your backstory merges with your partner's, becoming an integral part of all those conversations that make up the foundation of a relationship. And when you've been married to this same person for nearly fifty years then that relationship, and all its familial history on both sides, becomes one of your truly defining characters as well as a highly adjustable lens through which you see the rest of the universe. A family relationship also comes to be enriched by our professions, at least for those of us lucky enough by virtue of birth circumstances to have a profession. My life as a biology professor has provided everything and more than I ever thought possible for a post-WWII Oklahoma child who has resisted, with all his might, the problem of growing up. But Karen's involvement in the arts has been perhaps the most enriching aspect of our lives in Nebraska, and if there is a strong statement to be made about this state, indeed about the very word "Nebraska" as a metaphor for circumstances assumed to be culturally impoverished, then my first task is to dispel that notion.

For example, every day, while simply doing what college professors do as part of their job, I walk past, and could easily touch if I wanted to, sculptures by Richard Serra, Mark di Suvero, David Smith, and a dozen others with globally recognized names. There are at least five million residents of New York City who cannot make that claim. Numerous times over the past few years Karen and I have sat down to elegant dinners with Norman Geske, an eminent art historian, occasionally in places like Paris, France, and talked art for hours. There are at least seven million residents of New York City, and at least six billion other humans, who have never had such an experience, even once, and are never likely to have one. And we have had lunch with the Seacrests, listening to a budding opera star, just back from an international prize-winning gig in Europe, sing beside our table the overture from *Le nozze di Figaro* in honor of Rhonda and Jim's support of UNL's opera program. There are at least six million people in New York City who have never had a private and personal, tableside performance of Mozart's comic masterpiece, and at least another five billion people on Earth who do not know, or care, who Mozart was or what the fact of a human like Mozart, or Picasso, tells us about our species.

There are three pieces from these forty-three years as a biologist; their subjects are microscopic animals, western Nebraska, and my job, although I've given those chapters rather noble-sounding titles, considering their contents. "Through a Lens" is my summary of encounters with nature, especially microscopic nature, as a University of Nebraska–Lincoln faculty member. I've spent a whole lot of time looking at things very few others get to see, so I've tried to let you join me in the lab and share the lessons one learns from dealing with tiny creatures. "The Horse" is an excerpt from a book entitled *The Ginkgo: An Intellectual and Visionary Coming-of-Age*. This piece is likely to seem strange and even embarrassing, mainly because it deals with a man talking to a horse. The conversation is not the type that you usually associate with men and horses, so I've provided a short introduction, which is not a part of the original novel.

The Ginkgo is about the burdens of traditions. In this case, the traditions are those of the ranching life, and the necessary burdens, both behavioral and economic ones, run right up against the information age and Third-Millennium American values. *The Ginkgo* also is about what we learn from museums, painting, and sculpture. The book is a direct result of my encounters with the visual arts through Karen's work as Education Coordinator at the Sheldon Museum of Art and assigning papers to students in BIOS 101, most of whom arrive at UNL with a heavy load of backstory. A conversation with a horse is not exactly what comes to mind when one reflects on lessons learned from being married to Karen, participating in her life surrounded by the visual arts, and contemplating the burdens of tradition, but trust me, stranger connections have been made in the past and this one is legitimate. But you get to hear, and imagine, only a conversation with a horse. *The Ginkgo*, the book from which this piece is taken, is fiction, but written as if it were the literal truth; it's available as a trade paperback from Amazon and on Kindle.

"The Firm" deals with life as a faculty member at the University of Nebraska–Lincoln. At one time in the past, a colleague at another university suggested that I write a book entitled *The Department*, spilling all the secrets, insider information, and intrigue that comprise academic politics. It was quite a temptation, although liability issues prevailed and the only people who might be halfway interested in reading it were those who could have written it as easily as I. Nevertheless, there is something to be said about a business in which reputation is the currency, and especially about the way humans behave when our sense of self worth is defined only by what others say about us, especially behind our backs. Thus that last chapter in Part II is entitled "The Firm," a play on all the other works that have been so entitled, hopefully giving this title a somewhat sinister connotation.

Part III—A Future focuses on the next two millennia and the role played by scientific literacy in directing our behavior over those two thousand years. The pieces in Part III come straight out of my classroom presentations, my teaching and research—in the broadest sense—and related creative writing about science and the natural world. These essays, then, are a statement about what I *believe* I've learned from my career. In this section, you get a scientist's perspective on life as a member of the species *Homo sapiens* Linnaeus, 1758, but you also get one person's attempt to move beyond where he or she resides, intellectually, on a day-to-day basis. Part III is an attempt to use the knowledge gained from my research.

The vast majority of my everyday experience involves the lives of microscopic parasites: how they live, how they're transmitted, their reproduction and development, and their evolutionary relationships. But in addition to the daily research, planning experiments, backing up data, and designing figures for publication, a scientist's life also involves a constant engagement with larger questions about the scientific enterprise itself. We're always asking the question: what is the fundamental nature of this human activity we call "science"? So even as we're dissecting beetles, our thoughts drift off into the realm of planetary processes, the history of Earth, and the future of life on this only planet known to support it. The human condition is an integral part of this discussion; without humans there would be no awareness of the universe as we now understand the term, and I honestly believe that this awareness is an evolved trait.

Because evolution is the central unifying theme of biology, a biologist's mind constantly wanders from the Cambrian to the distant future, all the time wondering why others don't seem to have this intellectual affliction. I'm sure that physicists' minds routinely wander between the subatomic to the cosmic, chemists' minds regularly explore a bewildering array of molecular structures and their associated functions, and geologists' minds journey easily from the planet's molten core to its highest mountain ranges. Scientists go places, not only literally, but also mentally and metaphorically, places that a massive body of knowledge can take us. Part III—A Future is a product of this metaphorical travel, a projection into the future of what I've thought about, mainly since 1966, in my four labs—room 124 Bessey Hall, room 424 Manter Hall of Life Sciences, a converted storage closet in Cedar Point's Goodall Lodge north of Ogallala, and the Swallow Barn at Cedar Point Biological Station—while dissecting insects and fish and identifying and counting their parasites. I need to thank Karen, my wife of forty-eight years, for reading this manuscript carefully, more than once. The first two chapters are personal enough, and focused on her family, so that I felt she needed to give me permission to use the material. But Karen is also a perfectionist editor with a distinguished publishing career herself, and she certainly put her skills to use on *Pieces of the Plains*. Five students read, and commented on, some of the writing: Paige Ahart, Alaine Knipes, Gabriel Langford, Matt Bolek, and Ben Vogt; they are mentioned again in the chapter "Acknowledgments, Notes, and Sources." Finally, I would like to give my sincere thanks to Rhonda and Jim Seacrest for sponsoring the publication of this book. If it were in my power to take every one of the seven billion human beings on Earth, or maybe the four billion that are twenty-one years of age or older, and sit them down in a booth at The Olive Garden, order them a Stolichnaya martini on the rocks (with olives and a twist of lemon), then offer to publish any book they'd write, I would do it instantly. Then the world would be, I honestly believe, not nearly so violent and corrosive a place.

—*John Janovy, Jr.*
July, 2009

PART I

Oklahoma

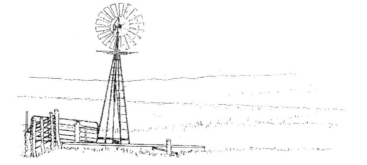

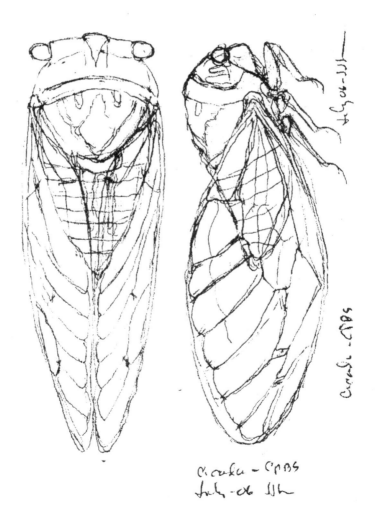

Cicada - CPBS
July - 06 SSh

Ethel

The sun is high now, and the day is hot ... Noon ...
Blue sky and breeze ... Gone.
—Peter Matthiessen, *Far Tortuga*

"These make me sad," she said, holding the photographic prints in her lap, by their edges so as not to put a smear on the surface. She slipped a fingernail behind the one she was studying, then slowly pulled it toward her, to see the next.

"Sad?"

Nostalgic is the proper word, she thought, but so formal, and so inadequate. So she said nothing. Her mother had died when she was a child. Many times she'd said that not everyone knew how it was to be a seven-year-old girl and have your mother die. Usually she made this comment late at night, maybe out on the highway, after a day at her stepmother's. Sometimes it was a holiday, or one of the many graduations, or births, when the clan descended on Grandmother Jenny and the food was carried out on big platters, mostly beef, ham, five-cup salad, steaming vegetables, and everyone sat around stuffing their faces and kidding the older boys about their girlfriends. Then it would be over. She would offer to help with the dishes, but Genevieve would say no, she'd do them later.

On the drive back is when she'd start talking about Jenny's courage, walking into that family of three girls and a working man, one of the girls just a baby, and accepting the responsibility. When their mother had died, the two older sisters had been sent for a time to their aunt and uncle's farm, out in the panhandle. There the western prairie's crackling summer dryness stamped its unforgiving mark on her memories. Never again would she see the smoke-green sage without saying that reminds me of Aunt Ethel's. A cicada in the August cottonwoods was a time machine—you could see it on her face the moment the chirring started its rise and fall: she was seven years old again, her mother had died, and she'd been sent with her older sister to stay with her aunt and uncle on a farm near the town of Woodward, Oklahoma.

Years later, the mother of two daughters, she felt drawn back to Woodward. An inner voice, it seemed, kept telling her a cycle of some kind wouldn't be complete unless her children saw the farm, walked through the buildings where she'd spent that indelible summer, and listened to the cicadas. He agreed to drive out to that part of the state, then bought black and white film for the trip. Farmsteads, he knew, were yin-yang places—on the one hand idyllic, romantic, full of worn angles and weathered lumber, the clutching emotions of a life obsessed with growth, a life among the calves, births, deaths, the grand elements of existence, and adoration of a God that giveth and taketh; on the other hand, hard work, grinding labor in the howling wind, hours upon a tractor, the prayer for rain answered by a swath of hail erasing in a few seconds a year's commitment to the land. Yes, a farm would be a place for black and white, contrasts. He would look for designs among the outbuildings, she could visit with Aunt Ethel, and the girls could play in the yard.

Outside, the familiar high plains dry heat came to him on a gentle wind. The woodlot was second growth, but the yard cottonwoods were gigantic. Only out here did they achieve their finest majesty—twisted by the gales, gray bark a woven matrix with wooden cords as thick as his arm. Down in the cracks he could see insects, microscopic lives scurrying into tiny canyons, away from delicate translucent spiders. A child could almost put her foot into one of those crevices, he thought, and use the cork ridges as steps into the branches, up where the cicadas sang. He let his imagination run on. The cicadas were calling her into an enchanted castle in the air. All she had to do was put her bare toes into the bark and take the first step, then the trunk would change into a spiral silver staircase. Desire, desire to get up to where the cicadas sang, a wish, a want, was the switch to change a cottonwood tree into silver stairs. She put her foot on the gnarled roots, felt the roughness, and turned her face, squinting, into the canopy.

She could not take the step. Her faith lay in other worlds. It was the song she needed, not the rattling scratchy frantic insect, the buzz bomb trapped by ornery hand, or a kingbird's beak, but the song. The song came with the soft knocking of waxy leaves against themselves, with the western Oklahoma summer heat, the stillness. She looked more closely at the trunk. Abandoned cicada skeletons still clung to the bark, split open at the back, the tangle of cast trachea like threads of a worn-out jacket. They had climbed out of the soil, emerged, let the magic drop of fluid stretch their wings, then flown into the swaying heights. He wondered how big this tree had been when she'd decided not to climb. Again this year there were cast skeletons, still clinging to the bark.

He'd often thought about the lives of cicadas, how they were a part of his own childhood, too, but not the same kind of part. His mother hadn't died when he was seven, and besides, in those days boys were supposed to be curious about squirmy things—toads, snakes, various "bugs"—but girls were supposed to be afraid. While he and a friend would spend the night with a flashlight watching the cicada emerge from its nymphal case, waiting for the wings to unfold and harden, saying to one another "if you touch it now, it'll never fly," she would lie in the afternoon back bedroom, surrounded by old furniture, listening to the rise and fall of the cicada's song, then the chorus of chirring, and wonder if her mother was in Heaven. For him, the insects were creatures of the night, the secret climb onto rough walls, or limbs, the agonizing ecdysis, the dark hours of soft flightless vulnerability, with finally the rattling dash into hiding, clutched beneath a twig high in the elms, when there were still elms in the city, with the morning warmth. His midnight flashlight, trained until the batteries died on the persistent imago, symbolized his relationship with the natural world. His excitement came with doing something nobody else did: watch the "locusts" at night, see them at important times, do what the birds could not do, peel away the protective darkness, watch the acquisition of flight, then smile, and go back to his bedroom while the world slept, stole, killed, writhed under the covers, and called it life, and ponder for a while before sleep the discoveries he'd made the hundredth time.

But for her, cicadas were creatures of the day, the afternoon, and they were markers of major events in human lives. She would never hear another one without expecting a change, usually one she could not control. She had an expression, a look of the past; she was the vulnerable one, the receiver, the one who responded; her thoughts were made by what happened to those around her. Thirty years, and if she lived that long sixty or seventy years, could go by, and anyone who'd been with her that summer in Woodward would be taken back there by the look on her face when she heard the cicadas. It's all gone, said the look, my childhood, my aunt and uncle, the farm, the physical assurance of a grandmother, and a mother, the carefree happiness of a little girl, the caring in times of sorrow, gone into the Oklahoma wind, gone with the leaves, paint on the barn, all gone except the cicadas.

She never wanted things to change. She wanted to stay a child, her own children to stay children, her parents to stay alive, and her aunts and uncles. She did not like death, did not consider it educational. But the world would not wait for her. The grinding politics of war, starvation, the clearing of vast forests, rivers sucked dry, chemicals poisoning the soil, drugs, schoolboy bullets in their classmates' brains, tangled shards of steel and blood and broken glass along the highway, missiles in a silo on the prairie, the hopeless clash of race, of religions, all came to her in an endless parade of "news." It never ended, this mess made of a lone world drifting in the outer arm of a commonplace galaxy. The cicadas sang. She did not want to go where the songs took her. The journey would erase all that had gone wrong since she was seven years old, but the songs also would erase everything that had gone right. From the paradox came the look on her face. The chirring in the heat said in falling rising words: good and bad; only one with the other.

Wandering among the buildings, he took some pictures. He knew they would not show what he had in his mind. In the negatives there was never enough contrast for him, never a fraction of that he could see in the gray boards, a rusted nail driven decades ago, the barbed wire hidden in a tangle of wild plum, all telling him of the hardest work and the deepest love for the land. The western prairies seemed to homogenize the landscape—one farmstead was the next, low hills were places to see more low hills, tree-lined creeks were snakes you passed while the radio played weather, local news, and markets. But weather and markets were the news. His contrast lay at a higher, more abstract, level, than his pictures could show. Somehow, he thought, if a person could work at the higher level, he could show the human experience on earth in a way that could not be seen otherwise. The yin and yang were not really in the deep shadows behind bleached boards of a loading chute; no, they lay in the constant battle of growth and death in a fertile land of a dying culture, in the elusive subtle complexity of a flat horizon over upright grass, in the native's rich visual world against the visitor shading his eyes in the glare, and in the timeless memories bound so tightly to the calling of an insect.

They'd walked through the buildings and empty pens together before she went inside to talk to Aunt Ethel, and he and the girls, bored, wandered back into the yard. She'd remembered the names of the cows. This hadn't surprised him. She remembered birthdays of nieces, nephews, towns where second and third cousins lived. He didn't have to ask whether she'd given the cows their names that summer when she was seven. They'd all been named well in advance of her mother's death. Ethel was the kind of person who would name cows. They were female; they worked hard to keep the family fed; they suffered in the drought and cold, the isolation; they grew old and weathered; their late winter coats were tattered. They did their duties, walked their paths worn, by habit and efficiency and their burden, into the prairie sod. Yes, Aunt Ethel would have named them all. He wondered if the cows answered when called, maybe hearing Ethel's strained voice through the blowing dust and turned their heads, trying hard to see. There were no longer any cows in these buildings. Plowing ran nearly to the fence. Except for the homestead itself, the land was leased. Ethel was free. Cicadas chirred. He called to the girls. He'd seen his picture and he needed them.

1 ETHEL

The driveway into the farmstead was dirt, or more properly, dust, sandy dust, in this part of the country. Tracks curved away from the blacktop, from the gravel on the shoulder where the mailbox stood, toward the woodlot, and then beneath the giant cottonwoods where lower limbs dragged their umbrella of leaves on small thin branches out over the lane. Late afternoon sun bounced off the sand, made him shield his eyes as he looked from the highway to the house.

"Run toward me, along the driveway. Race!" "Race" was a better word than "run," at least for a picture.

"Go!" He waited until they were halfway to him, then pressed the shutter.

"Who won?!" Breathless; laughing; yet, tense.

"I forgot to look."

Winning had not been the purpose of this race. But in all fairness, they could not have known that. He felt bad about not worrying who would win; he owed them the judgement for their efforts. On the other hand, nobody had thought to mark a finish line. Someone says "race" and off we go, not knowing where it will end, then ask someone else if we won. He refused to dwell too long on this jaundiced view of his world. They were on vacation. He was taking pictures of the family. The philosophy could wait for coffee break at work. But the dash down Ethel's driveway did not leave his mind gracefully. He turned his thoughts to the negative, the print. He was not really a photographer; he had great love for the negative, too little patience with the print. Maybe there was a lesson in that situation, too. He needed a beer and a nap. He walked to the house and got iced tea and a conversation about distant relatives instead.

The print was 8×10, on F5 paper, his own purposeful violation of some photographer's rule, or perhaps his own homage to an internal world of stark contrasts. He did not care; he was no professional with a camera; he made his living as a scientist and the image coming to him under the red safelight was art. He waited until there were two nearly black silhouettes beneath an equally dark cascade of boughs, shadows reaching out behind the running figures, all against the glaring path of tire tracks. The girls had lost their faces in his use of the chemicals, but the loss was somewhat of a gain. More yin-yang, he thought, then filed away for future times alone with his art the possibility that the western prairies were responsible for his mental processes.

How do people who live in the mountains think? he wondered. One mistake in the mountains and you fall past layered geological epochs, the timeless earth itself seeing you not as a person, but as one more potential fossil—*Archeopteryx* with a ballpoint in his pocket. Is this why the Swiss make such fine watches? Do it carefully, with precision, notice every small detail, if you are to live in the mountains? Unforgiving land breeds watchmakers. But on the prairies you walk forever, fall, and only the wind says try again, take another step, maybe you'll get further this time. Surely there is something to see on the prairies besides horizon and sky. The baby learns to catch flowers, ridges carved by intermittent streams, grasses lying low, and later the child watches geese, and such trees as are sculpted by the wind. There are no watchmakers on the prairies, he decided; too many options, too many opposite ways of seeing, too much change mixed with stability, to even need a watch. At home he studied the dry print. My own children, he said to no one, they've lost their faces in my use of light, chemicals on paper, but they've gained a certain timelessness. Two sisters once again race down a dusty path. The ancient cottonwoods smile to one another, and whisper: they're doing it again, they say, the girls are racing down the driveway, again.

He was satisfied with what he'd done. They'd made the pilgrimage to the farm at Woodward, satisfied someone's need to convince herself that she'd survived her mother's death. He had looked around the place, wondered what there was to be recorded for all eternity—was that not why you took a camera on vacation—and come away with the reason they'd gone to Aunt Ethel's in the first place. He could look at the picture of his children and see in it his wife and her sister as children dealing with a shattered world by racing down a couple of tire tracks in the prairie while the cicadas chirred and the cottonwoods stood smiling. But he had achieved nothing else.

1 ETHEL

That didn't bother him much; he understood himself well enough to know why he saved his most serious thinking for black and white film. He was a person of inner contrasts: the artist was always struggling with the scientist, the worker with the bum, the radical with the reactionary. But for him the opposite of "right" was not "wrong," it was "many shades of right." The opposite of "wrong" was not "right," but "wrong only in certain ways, or at certain times." He lived on a sliding scale of contexts. So he was not a man of color. Color had a story all its own. Colors lived in a different domain of reality from pure white light. So he was satisfied with his black and white print of two girls running under the trees. He could look at the picture and hear cicadas. But the prairie wind didn't whistle through his picture, the sand didn't move, the miles of blowing grass said nothing to him, and he knew why. Even as he smiled and said he didn't care, he remembered the wind and the horizon; they were in his mind. He didn't need a picture.

◆　　◆　　◆

In the beginning all the universe was within a point, a dot, and then the dot exploded. Fifteen billion years later, apes rise on their hind legs to think, then do the math that allows them to look backward to the beginning, to write books about the first three minutes, and the last three, and to predict the future ten billion years away. In all their efforts to erase time, the scientists have come full circle to the arts: their laws have shown a history. This is the way things behave, they say, and by "things" they mean small mites of energy. Then they build stars, and planets, on paper, and because they've built the planets, they consider themselves to have also made the prairie winds, cottonwoods, cicadas chirring on an August afternoon.

But once a mind has shown eternity to have a beginning and an end then the brain has put itself in the same category as fingers whose clutching at a shutter make one picture, one and only one, a phrase that sounds like math, or other theory. "Pretty," or "powerful," says some critic, or color-coded for my living room she says with checkbook in hand, but unique, he says from behind the lens, looking toward the edge of a vast land where no one falls down very far, stretching straight and flat to a distant horizon. The captured bit of time will be there for all to see, like a tiger in the zoo, proof of striped cats afoot in the jungle, because we caught one and put it in a cage. And how do we know the universe is old, that once it was young, and that some day it will die? He caught a piece, with his camera, and put it out for all to study. The piece he caught was there, once, and now is gone. Like the cicadas, and her childhood, her mother, Aunt Ethel's farm, the cows, two sisters racing down a path, it is gone. But here in her hand, when she looks at it, the chemicals on paper make her sad. And because she's sad, he knows the picture's good.

Afterword

This piece was originally written for a book of photographs by John Spence, a local artist friend and superb photographer. Virtually all of it is true. John walked into my office one day, laid a large envelope of his photographs on my desk, and asked if I would be interested in writing something to accompany them, perhaps for submission as a coffee table type book. Of course I agreed to try the writing without even looking at the pictures; I knew John and his work well enough to say "yes." Then I brought a stack of those photographs home for Karen to see, and she did indeed sit down in her living room chair, carefully slip her fingernail beneath the edges, and say "these make me sad."

With that statement, I knew immediately how to write the essay. We had visited Aunt Ethel's farm at Woodward years earlier, and I had taken the photograph of our two daughters racing down the driveway under the cottonwoods. And for each of the fifty years that Karen and I have either been dating, or engaged, or married, every time the cicadas start chirring in late summer, she comments that the sounds remind her of that summer at Woodward after her mother died. So this essay is actually about the tiny things that connect us with major life events, the almost invisible threads that are woven into our lives from the very beginning, and the way certain moments can direct our vision backward, toward those very small details we accumulate over time.

The Spence manuscript was written mostly in third person. I tried to put myself in his mind when he took the pictures. In looking back on my writing, painting, and scientific activities of the past six decades, trying to evaluate their quality, what they actually say about the universe, that Spence manuscript stands out as one of the pieces with which I am most personally satisfied. Naturally it was rejected over and over again, and the photo-essay project never saw the light of day. One of the essays in it did eventually get published, however, appearing in my book *Dunwoody Pond* as the chapter entitled "The Road to Roscoe." *Dunwoody Pond* gathered only three or four reviews, none of which was in my local newspaper, the Lincoln *Journal Star*. But one of the *DP* reviews, I've forgotten from where, singled out that chapter—"The Road to Roscoe"—as being "particularly riveting." Those two words seemed to validate my own assessment of the material. I have been a guest speaker at gatherings where, while being introduced, my host reads sections from that particular chapter. I am still very satisfied with the Spence manuscript, regardless of its ultimate fate.

Someone is likely to read this last paragraph then react in the cynical, sarcastic, way that pseudo-intellectuals, especially those in positions of power, often react when a writer claims that something is among his or her best work. Anyone who has produced anything original, be it art, music, literature, or science, knows how difficult it is to actually assess serious original work at the time it is produced. And anyone who has produced an original work has first, if not the only right to judge its quality. The quality, or lack thereof, that others attribute to the work is all in the others' minds or, some believe, in the marketplace. Sometimes when students, especially the pre-meds, are uncomfortable passing judgment on their own work, I suggest playing the role of Dr. Paul Gachet in Auvers-sur-Oise, France, and imagining that during an appointment with your patient Vincent van Gogh, he's just declared "one of my pictures will sell for $40 million" (or the equivalent in French francs at the time.) Such a declaration would do nothing to dilute your opinion that van Gogh was crazy. Remember, however, that van Gogh thought Gachet was even crazier than he was.

The Woodward farm is gone, now, at least as a family enterprise with which I have any connection by marriage, although the land itself is still in production, farmed by members of the large Campbell family, next door neighbors for nearly a century. If a writer living throughout the Great Plains has anything to say about his or her nation's evolution from a personal perspective, it's a commentary on the demise of the family farm, not so much as an economic unit, but as a cultural one. This claim may be a stretch, but the cultural loss is, I believe, manifested in the majority of today's college students who are ignorant of rat, or for that matter any vertebrate's, internal anatomy and who are startled by what they find when they dissect a freshly killed one in biology lab.

Our vision of Farmer Jones in his overalls, smiling in pastoral bliss beside his barn, is the stuff of old children's books. Nowadays, Farmer Jones may still be in his overalls, but individual producers—farmers and ranchers—must become skilled accountants, diversify their operations, and increase their holdings in order to maintain a family business in any kind of healthy condition. The literal homestead as an ideal, a metaphor for the American dream, is as gone as that day beneath the cottonwoods at Aunt Ethel's, but the concept remains, morphed into every entrepreneur's startup loan, remodeling of an old building, printing of stationery, and uncrating the inventory. Indeed, this metaphorical homestead is almost a defining character of a powerful nation founded by people seeking relief from religious oppression, venturing across a treacherous ocean in surprisingly small ships, and staking claim to a bountiful land occupied by aborigines. The very word "American" carries with it an assumption of risk, adventure, and freedom to win or lose at any of life's games, no matter where those games are played, even five miles south of Woodward, Oklahoma.

The statistical disappearance of the family farm, and the nuclear family committed to it on site, obtaining all their sustenance from its activities, is well documented in United States Census records from the past century. The land remains, of course, but use of that land is increasingly mechanized and corporate. Between 1940 and 2000, the number of American farms dropped from about 6.3 million to around 2 million—that's a loss of four million individual businesses over the productive lifetime of one farmer—while the average size of the remaining farms increased from 140 acres to 471. That documentation, the *de facto* disappearance of people from vast regions of the central prairies, led to one of our more interesting, relatively controversial, evolutionary ideas promulgated by Deborah and Frank Popper, a couple of Easterners with PhDs and described with a rather infective catchphrase: "Buffalo Commons." The idea was perceived by many as simply allowing this part of the world to return to its original state, but in fact the Poppers saw a much larger process, a "softer" evolution of the prairie biome into a more "natural" economic system in which bison could, if not should, play an economic role.

The life, experience, and as yet unfixed fate of this two-word phrase—Buffalo Commons—comprise a model for our evolving nation, a device for achieving a certain level of understanding about the way our United States of America operates. Although it's a somewhat roundabout approach to explaining why Buffalo Commons has such metaphorical staying power, we might begin this explanation with the birth of Thomas Sidney Lucas on April 29, 1872, in Mt. Pulaski, Illinois. Twenty years later, in Winfield, Kansas, Thomas married Lillian Marie Hoge, a year and four months his senior. Tom failed to stake a claim in the 1893 land run, but he and Lily Lucas nevertheless established a homestead in Woodward County, buying a 160-acre "relinquishment" from a local "Mr. Horn." Like many settlers, Tom quickly built a one-room sod house in the northeast quarter of Section 23, Township 22 North, and Range 21 West. Six children resulted from this marriage—Mildred, Claudie, Ivan, Ethel, Emmett, and Evelyn, in that order; all must have helped with chores and learned about birth, death, and weather from firsthand experience.

Ethel was born on September 18, 1897. She later married Ferris Campbell, one of the Woodward Campbell clan's many landowners, and moved to his farm east of the Lucas property.

Evelyn, the youngest, was born July 15, 1908. She eventually married Glenn T. Oneth, a mechanic from Jet, Oklahoma (2000 population, 230, including 113 males and 117 females), with whom she produced three girls—Dolores, Karen, and Wanda Sue, in that order—then died in surgery for an intestinal blockage in El Reno, Oklahoma, on March 14, 1948. Evelyn was forty years old at the time of her death. When Evelyn died, Karen, Wanda Sue, and Dolores were sent to Aunt Ethel and Uncle Ferris' farm. There the western prairie's crackling summer dryness would stamp its unforgiving mark on Karen's memories. Never again would she see the smoke-green sage without saying "that reminds me of Aunt Ethel's." Then John Spence would go out into a rural prairie landscape, take some photographs, and bring them to Karen's husband's office. These pictures would find their way home, into her lap, where she would look at them one by one, holding them by their edges so as not to smear the surface, slipping a fingernail behind the one she was studying, then slowly pulling it toward her to see the next, and saying "These make me sad."

The idea of returning vast regions of the Great Plains to wilderness, presumably occupied only by bison, prairie dogs, coyotes, rattlesnakes, meadowlarks, pocket gophers, a dozen species of perennial grasses, cottonwoods and willows along the stream beds, and red-tailed hawks, is an intriguing one, especially to people who don't live in rural Oklahoma, Kansas, Nebraska, eastern Colorado, or the Dakotas. Those of us in this part of the country still tend to think of ourselves in terms of this wildlife occupying our signature landscape, even if that landscape is found only in a nature preserve far outside of town. But a 532-mile drive from Lincoln, Nebraska, to Willis, Oklahoma, a drive I take every year as part of my job, does not necessarily reveal a disappearing rural America. Instead, there is a defined set of houses, outbuildings, machinery, silos, and livestock pens, all landmarks that tie the Buffalo Commons into a single unit, at least in the mind of a person taking this trip. Some of these structures need paint; others have been painted recently. Children's ride toys suggest changes in the lives of residents rarely seen as I pass their homes at a mile a minute. Over the years, mailboxes acquire stylized purple cat heads; the kid who once used that plastic Big Wheel now goes to Kansas State University and his ride toy is probably a full-sized pickup. Once in a while there is a yellow ribbon tied around a tree. Someone has gone to war. People are in fact living and working in this vast, open, water-challenged, environment. The infrastructure that allows these lives to be pursued would be considered science fiction by Lillian (Hoge) and Thomas Lucas, Aunt Ethel and Uncle Ferris, could these folks suddenly be resurrected and plopped down in the Buffalo Commons armed only with their knowledge and experience earned at the hands of the Kincaid Act. As a minimum, that infrastructure consists of genetic research on strains of wheat, genetically engineered seed corn, computer programs to control center pivot sprinklers, the global commodities market and political machinations that control it, startup biotech companies, pesticide chemists battling insecticide resistance (itself strong evidence for evolution), a highly complex set of agricultural subsidies and regulations negotiated by elected officials whose first hand knowledge of rural America is, at best, lost in childhood, the prime interest rate, a food processing industry so intensely competitive that it almost redefines the word "competition," dietary fads, and an occasional cow exhibiting symptoms of bovine spongiform encephalopathy, a single animal that can set off a worldwide economic blaze not unlike that real fire started by one of Kate O'Leary's five, all of which, we must surmise, were named, but none of whose names survive.

Were they still alive, Ferris Campbell and Tom Lucas would be on the Internet daily and their respective wives might well be owners of a cottage information technology company. Within minutes, if not seconds, Ferris and Tom, plunked down at their new laptops with their 500GB hard drives, 16GB memory, and 2.66GHz processors (by the time you read this, these figures will be passé!) could easily discover that the very term, "Buffalo Commons," and the idea it conveyed, had already morphed into a variety of forms: a serious attempt to actually produce one (Great Plains Restoration Council), a McCook, Nebraska, folk arts and storytelling festival, a futuristic sci-fi military command, a mathematical exercise in the solving of complex and ill-defined problems developed by Bernard Hollister, an Illinois Mathematics and Science Teacher Academy Master Teacher who "passionately believed that a teacher's role is to stimulate the natural curiosity of students to investigate, question and learn," and copyrighted by the Illinois Mathematics and Science Academy's Center for Problem-Based Learning, a birding tour guide industry, a "weblog devoted to books, authors, and readers on the Great Plains of North America," along with links to booksellers' own web pages, a bison hunting operation with a professional guide, a title of a poem, an Oklahoma geographer's assertion that he'd originated the idea, an anti-bioterrorist training exercise conducted by the North Dakota Department of Health, and a Virginia Wesleyan Student's description of the difficulty of solving this problem in a class designed to teach problem solving in general. What is this problem that seems such an ideal teaching device? It is the problem of how to manage essential natural resources in a wise manner at the national level in the modern world. Everyone has an idea; nobody, not even a student at a small university, has a solution acceptable to all. That's why "Buffalo Commons" has, as they say in the advertising business, legs.

John Spence took his photographs before the Poppers published their idea.

Bohemian Coffee Cake

Radio 1950

8 C Flour
5 eggs (well beaten)
1 C cream (heated)
1 oz yeast (disolved in 1/4 C water)
1 C butter
1 C sugar
1 C milk (scalded) (cool)

1/8 t mace
1 t grated lemon rind
2 t salt
1 C raisins
1 C nuts prefrably almonds

Blend flour and butter (as for pie crust) add eggs. Add sugar to cream (heated) Soak yeast in 1/4 C cold water then add to cool milk. Add balance of ingredients. except raisins, nuts + lemon rind. Let rise 1 1/2 hrs punch down. Add remaining ingredients and let rise again Then roll dough 1/2" thick. Cut into 9 strips. Twist four together braid 3 and twist 2. Place on top (butter) of each other. Let rise a little while, brush top with egg beaten with cream added. Pat on a baking sheet and bake 1 1/4 hrs at 300° Glaze while still warm with a thin icing of powdered sugar + cream. Decorate with candied fruit if desired. Yield two large or four small cakes.

Genevieve

The last of all familiar ties that bind
The new tame empire to the rough old days.

—Kenneth Kaufman, *The Last Stand*

Genevieve lay dying. She'd ended up in the intensive care unit on a Friday in May with congestive heart failure. The doctors called her son. Any papers that need signing? Get them signed. Then she lived through the weekend. One by one the stepdaughters and stepgrandchildren arrive, spend their few allotted minutes with Genevieve, say their goodbyes, and go back to the ICU waiting room. Between trips in to see Genevieve, they talk with other ICU temporary residents, thrown together like strangers on a crippled airliner, bonding, sharing personal stories, leaving half-finished packages of cookies. One man's wife, a cancer patient, has been in ICU since October. Someone asks him how much it was costing. Millions, he said; probably millions. When it's May, and your wife's been in intensive care since October, and you've spent most of your days and nights in the waiting room, then the cost of her care evidently moves off the list of taboo subjects. The place is littered not only with food packages, but also with Christian reading material. Periodically a white telephone rings. Through taking phone messages, visitors quickly learn each other's names. Through talk fueled mostly by stress, boredom, and a common sense of empathetic helplessness, visitors quickly start sharing life and family stories.

May turns to June, and June turns to Oklahoma. Outside the Midwest Regional Medical Center, near Tinker Air Force Base in Midwest City, the heat is oppressive, moist. When Genevieve drifts off into fitful sleep for hours at a time, Dolores, the oldest stepdaughter, her husband Ferrill, and Karen, the middle child, go sightseeing around the hospital, looking for places to have lunch. At some point they drive through residential streets, following the same path as the May 3 tornado. Afterward they talk about a school bus that was twisted like a washcloth you're wringing, people who couldn't find their houses because all the other houses were gone and there were no reference points. I drive down to join the death watch and get the tornado tour. Tornadoes pick up mud and vegetation and roll them up into fist-sized balls. When these wet, adobe-like, balls get thrown around at 300 miles per hour, they stick to your house, Ferrill explains. One brick wall is covered with red balls of mud and grass. The brick wall next to it is missing. Talk turns to the salvage company. They make a living off disasters, someone says. Early June turns to late June, and Genevieve is still alive. We start talking about October, how much longer the man's wife could last. Then the doctors start planning for Genevieve to go home. Home is El Reno, 26 miles west of Oklahoma City. Nobody knows what to do with her when she gets home.

◆　　◆　　◆

Life on the American prairies is characterized first and foremost by straight roads and distant horizons. Out in the grain belt, only deep-cut creek beds are hidden away by big trees; the rest of this landscape is pretty obvious and easily characterized, at least from a distance. When we moved to Nebraska, in 1966, we thought: fine; a nice place to rear our kids, a long day's drive from Oklahoma—far enough to keep our distance, near enough to get home for Christmas—a decent job, freedom, elbow room. The problem of Kansas, that it lies in between Oklahoma and Nebraska, in between the place where we grew up and the place we'd chosen to make a new life, really didn't manifest itself too strongly until mid-December. We learned quickly how weather becomes a character in prairie, no less than in coastal, lives. And when weather becomes a character in everyone's life, then it also becomes a character in prairie music, prairie art, prairie literature, and prairie business.

It wasn't until we started commuting across Kansas, paying last respects, burying, or at least preparing to bury, parents, that the hours from Washington to South Haven along State Highway 15 turned into a time of thinking, reflection back on the dozens of journeys through snow, ice, torrential storms, searing heat, magnificent sunsets, welcome sunrises, together comprising a forty-three-year lesson on appreciation of nature at its best and worst, the familiar stability of a single barn west of the road, various automobiles, and evolution of a childhood home studied from afar. "Going to Oklahoma" became synonymous with return, or at least a good attempt at returning, to a cultural womb. Such are my thoughts across Kansas, driving to visit Genevieve on a deathbed, which thanks to the "miracles of modern medicine" is rapidly becoming her life bed.

In early November she's in her living room, constant home care provided by former students she'd taught in grade school. She can't last until Thanksgiving, one of them says. We enter through the garage; the door is always open; nobody steals anything from that garage, and if they did, everyone would instantly recognize where the moldy *Reader's Digest* books and rusted 1940s hand tools came from. Thanksgiving comes and goes. In mid December, Karen, the middle child who's been commuting across Kansas, sends her stepmother a gigantic poinsettia. A week later, she's wondering what to send Genevieve for Christmas. What do you send a person who is completely confined to a hospital bed in her living room, and who can move only her hands and head, but whose piercing blue eyes are as clear and sharp as the day she was born eighty-six years ago? What do you send a person for Christmas when she's not supposed to live until Christmas, a person who married your father fifty years ago, after his beautiful young wife died following surgery, then took on the responsibility of his three young girls, rearing them as her own?

There is no answer to this question. Karen makes a Bohemian coffee cake, one of Genevieve's family recipes, and puts it in express mail, along with some chocolate chip cookies. Those caregiver ladies—the former grade schoolers—will appreciate it, she says. She knows her stepmother will appreciate the idea more than the coffee cake and cookies; Genevieve has been clamping her mouth shut, resisting all nourishment, for weeks. In the middle of Kansas, conversation often turns to the question of how long it takes a terminally ill person to starve herself to death. At least she's not in pain,

Karen says. There's no external evidence she's in pain, I reply, watching a red-tailed hawk lift off a pole south of Abilene.

Christmas in El Reno, Oklahoma, was always, first and foremost, an attack upon Bohemian coffee cake. The blue-eyed woman who can move only her head and hands won't be able to eat more than a few crumbs at best, if she will even unclamp those dentures and try, but the symbolism of Bohemian coffee cake will be obvious and she will understand why it was sent. Karen's sister, Wanda Sue—"Susie"—also makes a Bohemian coffee cake and takes it to her step-mother's kitchen. Back in the years when all our families were young, when all the children were still small enough to crawl up on their grandfather Papper Glenn's lap and kiss him for dollar bills, Genevieve started making Bohemian coffee cakes beginning shortly after Thanksgiving and continued through Christmas, making sure to have a gigantic one laid out when all the relatives came home.

I don't remember which grandchild started calling Glenn Oneth "Papper;" it might have been our eldest, Cindy, the verbal one, at some age when children are not supposed to talk in complete sentences but when Cindy nevertheless was putting strings of words together rather assertively, usually in short commands or summary judgements—*Regular one gallon please. Shampoo on it sounds very bad.*—regardless of whether she also provided the necessary surrounding context. I don't know what the other grandchildren called Glenn, but we called him Papper, to distinguish him from my father, Popper, a name definitely bestowed by Cindy. After the kids all kissed Glenn's bald head on Christmas day, and got their dollars, then the grownups got their chances, but for $5 bills. Then we'd go back to the coffee cake.

Dolores, the oldest stepdaughter, and her husband Ferrill; their four offspring, in order of production—Patrick, Paula, Phil, and Perry; Karen the middle stepdaughter, her husband John, and their children Cindy, Jenifer (Jena), and John III; Wanda Sue (Susie), the baby stepdaughter, and her husband Lou, later divorced, Wendy, their oldest, then Wade and Wesley, the fraternal twins; Glenn Edwin (Eddie), Genevieve's only true child, and his wife Susie, along with their two— Amanda and Ashley. This was the basic crowd that needed

Genevieve's Bohemian coffee cake in order to make Christmas legitimate. Later, as various kids moved through appropriate ages, there were girlfriends and boyfriends, some later turning into wives and husbands, and they also needed Bohemian coffee cake.

This almost Biblical list of Oklahoma begats has no larger significance beyond the reminder that personal history is a genetic heritage of being born human. Cro-Magnons must have had their own version of Bohemian coffee cake, as must the Sumerians, and the Cherokee. Details are not important; generalities are extremely so. How long Karen waits before punching down the dough matters greatly to Karen, but matters not at all to humanity. If we believe the media, the fact that Karen makes Bohemian coffee cake at Christmas for a mother who's unable to eat more than a crumb also matters not at all to humanity. If we believe what we tell ourselves via our common voice—television and Internet—then what's important to humanity is the size of Manny Ramirez's baseball contract, number of Israelis killed by the latest rockets from the Gaza Strip, number of American soldiers killed in the latest Baghdad car bomb, and "the Dow." But when a society stops making Bohemian coffee cake at Christmas just because a mother is supposedly dying, then that society is dying, too. And when sisters stop vying for a mother's attention, then something's fundamentally wrong; a bit of our common humanity, that humanness we share with even our most violent enemies is gone. So naturally, with both Karen's and Wanda Sue's Bohemian coffee cakes gracing the kitchen bar next to where Genevieve lies in her hospital bed living on and on, the discussion turns to which one is best.

This discussion is actually a continuation of the discussion of which stepdaughter's poinsettia is prettiest. Wanda Sue, who lives in Yukon a few miles away from El Reno, a town with "Home of Garth Brooks" painted on the water tower, raises the subject first. She visits Genevieve, assesses both the poinsettias and the coffee cakes then calls us.

"She wouldn't say which one was best," says Wanda Sue "Susie."

"Did she say which poinsettia was the prettiest?"

"No."

But Karen knows hers was the prettiest. At least it was the biggest. When judging poinsettias for quality, I always recommend size. When it comes to cultured plants, size is a measure of success at nourishing a living organism; beauty is genetic luck of the draw. The same rule probably applies to people, although size is probably more a measure of Bohemian coffee cake input than of general nourishment, and beauty, while still a genetic fortuity, can be expressed in thousands of ways not available to vegetation.

Genevieve's reaction to these coffee cakes and poinsettias is not too difficult to discern: it's an acknowledgement of intent. When you're 86, able to move only hands and eyes, starving yourself to death, and your stepchildren send poinsettias and Bohemian coffee cake, then you know Christmas has been laid bare, stripped of all pretensions, with only unwrapped tradition to give and receive. These plants and coffee cakes are a combination of permanence and ephemerality. Neither will last very long, but neither will ever die as long as there are humans to keep alive the acts of making and giving. Their bodies will age, wither, wilt, or in the case of Bohemian coffee cake undergo the biochemical transformations necessary to convert it into energy and excrement. And because poinsettias are a "symbol" of Christmas, the plants sitting in Genevieve's dark living room represent the idea that there is a life hereafter, an idea kept alive only by believers just like commercially available *Euphorbia pulcherrima*—poinsettias—are kept alive by greenhouse wizards carrying out the rituals of scheduled watering, pruning, light and darkness. The real difference between the idea and the plant, of course, is that *E. pulcherrima* exists in the wild in Mexico, quite oblivious of humans or Christmas.

The coffee cakes, however, have no independent germ line; they have to be made from scratch, each December, and only in December, and only because Genevieve made them. Their untouched presence on the dining room table now laden with magazines and newspapers read a hundred times by caregivers, speaks first of honor, second of respect, and third of challenge. Genevieve recognizes the honor; her eyes give it all away. She knows her stepchildren make coffee cakes because she made them, and she knows their children will try to make coffee cakes because her stepchildren made them. No form of honor surpasses this act of trying to do something just because someone else did it. Humans have no more valuable earthly resource than their own time, their own talents, their own unique way of sifting flour, cutting in shortening, buttering a baking pan, wiping their hands on the communal kitchen towel hanging from the designated drawer handle. To commit those most valuable resources, spending them in the ways someone else spent them, and for exactly the same reasons, is the highest form of honor.

Respect is for the art, in which resides the difficulty—or vice versa—of making Bohemian coffee cakes, and for the only somewhat predictable, thus individual, indeed the highly individual, outcome of each attempt. In a sense, every Bohemian coffee cake is a reminder of the deep emotional investment, the sustained and Herculean effort, the massive resource commitment, and the unpredictable outcome, of bearing, or otherwise taking responsibility for, a child. These cakes are a reminder that we cannot always bend nature—in this case yeast, flour, butter, all variable as only fungi, grass, and cattle can be—in precise ways. It's a rather transparently metaphorical ritual: a woman's hands, punching down the dough, deciding how to divide it, how gently to roll it, the directions she'll braid it, the final adjustment of shape, and how close to put the siblings on a baking sheet, then stepping back, having done all she can do within the powers given to her by birth and training, to watch the product rise in the oven, and finally, to be presented to a judging world.

Genevieve did all she could do with the raw products delivered into her hands by the quirks of fate. They all turned out as different as the two coffee cakes sitting untouched on a mahogany veneer table in a darkened room. You can tell they're sisters by their father's genes showing in their eyes, around their mouths. You can tell they're Genevieve's stepdaughters not only by their Bohemian coffee cakes, but also by their total faith in the powers of discipline, temperance, and deference to higher purpose. Glenn and his young wife Evelyn were the yeast, the flour, the milk, butter, and salt. Then Evelyn died suddenly and unexpectedly. Genevieve picked up the task, punched down the dough, divided it when ready, rolled it, braided it, took it out of the oven at exactly the right moment, then stepped back for the product to be judged by a world that had no part in, and no responsibility for, its making.

The challenge is between the sisters, but it's not much of a contest; none of the three really gets angry if she loses at Bohemian coffee cake. But they compete, nevertheless, knowing that coffee cake is but a harmless reflection of whatever ways they may have found to elbow one another for Genevieve's attention in the late 1940s and through the 1950s—the formative years for both stepchildren and step-mother. There were, of course, different outcomes of this more deeply biological game of familial interactions. Dolores was ten, Karen was seven, and Wanda Sue was not yet two when their mother died. Some time in the late 1940s, somebody sat the three sisters down for a formal photograph: Dolores on the left, Karen in the middle, and Susie on the right, three smiling, innocent, healthy children that could have been any three sisters anywhere in the First World.

Forty-five years later, they once again sit for a similar picture. They are no longer innocent, and they've put on a couple of pounds, but they are still smiling. Whatever health problems they've discovered in those four decades are not evident from the photograph. But the two older ones can never look at either picture without saying: Susie was always the baby, meaning, of course, that she was always treated with a certain amount of deference and patience by a stepmother whose maternal instincts were stimulated most strongly by a small voice, large dark eyes, and the fact that Wanda Sue was still small enough to sit on someone's lap.

Glenn Edwin—Eddie—Genevieve's only real child, doesn't make Bohemian coffee cakes. He builds cars instead, from scratch, like coffee cakes are built. Eddie's son Ashley not only builds cars, he races them. Eddie's wife and Ashley's mother is also Susie, "the other Susie;" she's the first thing that pops into my mind when I see a young man with a race car. Genevieve's condition—helpless to alter events—makes me think of mothers' reactions to sons' dangerous hobbies, mothers' reactions to sons and daughters in the military, and mothers' reactions to global events that send their children into combat. I don't remember Genevieve ever expressing any worries about her own son regardless of whatever he happened to be doing. In my earliest memories of Eddie he's dismantling a bicycle. Coaster brake parts are lying out on a newspaper on the sidewalk in various stages of greasiness. At some time later, he's riding the same bicycle. Few bikes have coaster brakes on them anymore. Today's bicycles are high-tech metallurgical miracles. But we've lost something when young boys trying to be men cannot get their first taste of humiliation at the hands of a machine by trying to reassemble a coaster brake. I wasn't around Ashley when he was at that formative mechanical age, but I'd not be surprised to learn that he started, successfully, on a really old bicycle.

Nowadays, Glenn Edwin has a full mechanical shop on a piece of land behind his house; the shop has enough equipment for Eddie to start with a 1957 Chevrolet frame and end up with an entry driven both to and in some classic car show 500 miles away in Omaha. Ashley's race car is in the garage attached to the house, the real garage, the garage where people are supposed to park their family car. This vehicle is no Winston Cup beauty, of course, and it has no sponsors' names covering every square and dented inch. Instead, it's a high school kid's response to the fact that his grandfather was, and his father is, a superb mechanic, plus the fact that there is a fully equipped car-building facility right behind his house.

On one of the visits, I'm shown the car. I didn't know Ashley raced, I say; isn't it dangerous? Eddie answers in a tone that tells me not everyone in the family approves of this avocation. He could be dealing drugs and carrying a handgun, I think; there are worse things, more dangerous things, than building your own race car and testing it against guys from several counties around on a Friday night dirt track. What's he going to do when he graduates, I ask. He wants to be a cop, says Eddie. In my mind, Genevieve is out at the dirt track cheering for her grandson instead of sleeping on a hospital bed in her living room, attended by care givers who were her elementary students thirty years earlier.

Back in Oklahoma City, my own stepparents—Rachel and Sam Bristow—ask about Genevieve's condition. Karen tells them the same story she's told anyone who wanted to know about the woman she calls mother, knowing full well that her biological mother rests beneath the dusty high plains west of Woodward. We sit in the living room of a house my father bought during the time he was figuring out that he was terminally ill, so that Rachel would need a home that met their rather substantial standards of quality. Those standards required a certain visual experience, a traffic flow, a sense of place, and of course a yard whose vegetation could be shaped according to an image in the mind of a man who constantly studied nature.

My father married Rachel about a year after my mother died, from cancer, at the age of forty-nine. This house is the third of those bought by Rachel and my father, and is one of two owned by Rachel and my stepfather Sam, one of my father's former business associates. Sam's own wife also succumbed to cancer, and eventually he and Rachel started seeing one another, then got married. Sam thus acquired a full set of grown children and grown grandchildren. Rachel was not only my father's insurance agent, but mine, too; after reading her name on my car policy, I finally got to meet her. They then sold their respective houses and bought a perfect home not too far from their previous homes. Eventually an expressway was built through that part of the city, so they moved further north and west, to the second of their new houses, in a subdivision called Quail Creek, on ground where I'd hunted rabbits as a boy.

As we had driven north on May avenue to see this second new home, we passed the corner of May and Britton Road, about a mile north of the small frame house on Elmhurst Avenue where many years earlier, from the security of my childhood bedroom on the east end, when both of my biological parents were still alive, during late summer I daily fired a water pistol through the screen at a large wasp nest in a nearby rose bush. God help anyone who might have accidentally wandered around that corner of our house during one of these sessions. Later, having outgrown that pursuit, I wandered the neighborhood with my BB gun, and then an air rifle, and eventually a shotgun, which meant I had to get beyond civilization in order to kill things, so with a friend, had walked north, along May avenue, eventually to Britton Road, past the

Wiley Post Airport, then on past Lake Hefner to what is now Quail Creek. At the time, there was an old two-pump filling station with a little wooden building at that corner, and my mother used to stop there periodically for gasoline. One day she pulled in there and within seconds two men tumbled out the door slugging one another. She sped away. The car was a black, 1940, four-door Ford.

Usually when my best friend, Ronnie Hall, and I walked past May and Britton Road, we stopped into that same filling station for candy. At the time, there was another fight going on, half a world away, and we watched its progress on the newspaper clippings tacked to the inside wall. The South Korean army, with its American allies, was being pushed steadily southward. Week by week, Ronnie and I would carry our shotguns past that corner, buy some candy, note the southward-moving line of battle, then go do our own battle with the Oklahoma cottontails. Eventually the line stopped moving. I distinctly remember the term "Pusan perimeter." My memories of WWII were of nothing but victory, and a treasured book of Bill Mauldin cartoons. The periodic check on Korea seemed like something unnatural: a defeat. Viet Nam, Iraq, and Afghanistan were still well into the future.

But the Korean War lesson about land was not lost on my fifteen-year-old mind. If at the time someone had told me that Oklahoma City would eventually absorb Wiley Post Airport, that little gas station, and fifteen or twenty more square miles of prime rabbit hunting territory—in a manner somewhat akin to the changes in Korean political geography—I might well have believed that person. Forty, almost fifty, years later, driving to and from Midwest Regional Medical Center for my visits to Genevieve and the ICU, it seems the unspoken prophecy has come true. Concrete and asphalt are everywhere except El Reno. When she "goes home," Genevieve will return to a town only slightly touched by the aggressive sprawl now spreading, almost malignantly, across central Oklahoma.

Back in the Intensive Care Unit, I hand Genevieve a *Time* magazine. It lies on her lap, out of deference to the intent, but she doesn't have her glasses, so thus unread. In all the holidays we'd spent in that house in El Reno, I'd never seen a *Time*, or, for that matter, any other weekly newsmagazine. So why would I buy her one now? Why would I assume she might like one in intensive care? The act is a result of my own frustration with ICU, the inevitable vision of me lying here instead of Genevieve, and reacting to the surroundings, the people, but most of all the values inherent in this high tech medical enclave. A television set hangs from the wall. A soap opera drones on. I ask Genevieve whether the hospital has cable, whether she has a remote. She shakes her head; inane electronic banter from one of the three commercial Oklahoma City channels is her background noise. An IV is plugged into her arm; tubes run from her nose; a catheter drains into a bag at the foot of her bed. There is a steady parade of color-coded hospital personnel in and out of her room. ICU is an intellectual wasteland. Genevieve is sealed off against traffic, diesel smoke, bird songs, the sounds of kids splashing in a pool or the morning paper hitting her porch, the smell of old library books and bacon cooking, the feel of worn carpet on her bare feet, the texture of houseplant leaves. No flowers are allowed in ICU. She can't even get the Holy Roller televangelists, MTV, ESPN, or a 24-hour per day shopping channel. No one reads the Bible to her, no one recites Shakespeare, and no one argues politics.

"Life" in the ICU makes this one visitor set aside all thoughts of business and wrestle with the very definition of "life." I've often marveled at the compelling success of television's medical programs. My notes don't reveal whether the Midwest Regional ICU waiting room TV is showing such material, although hospitals are such a common setting for today's "drama" that it would not have surprised me to be watching a fictitious version of what was going on behind the walls of that very building. I have this vision of people—of all walks of life, in all economic circumstances, everywhere throughout my nation's cities and rural hinterlands—glued to *General Hospital*. Somebody is being saved. Somebody's "life" is hanging in the balance.

Nobody ever asks whether this patient has headphones with a Mozart CD, nobody ever asks whether the nurse has arrived to read passages from E. O. Wilson, no frantic resident demands Picasso prints for the walls or wants to know the scientific names of flowers down in maternity. Instead, we see and hear the rush for defibrillators, catheters, scalpels and scissors, blood. Vicariously we join this team racing to save a "life." Cut to commercials. At two minutes 'til the hour suddenly there are smiles. Relatives are relieved, of course; but nothing from which a human "life" is constructed has actually been shown, demanded, or given. No memories, no sense of a difficult job completed satisfactorily by the patient, no daily tingle of a child practicing the piano, no new puppy, no baseball. Only people in medical garb holding medical gear.

The Midwest Regional Medical Center is a very large hospital next to an exceedingly large military establishment: Tinker Air Force Base, Oklahoma's biggest single-site employer and the world's largest aircraft repair facility. Like all such installations, Tinker has a full range of services from grocery stores, movie theaters, golf courses, and libraries to its own police force and fire department. Tinker also has a company college, Webster University, offering degrees in administration, computer resources, and information management. Enrollment in Webster University classes is open to military personnel, including retired ones, members of the National Guard and Reserves, civilian employees of and contractors working for the Department of Defense, and all legal dependents of all these groups.

Included among the 13,000 assigned personnel and another 10,000+ Tinker employees are members of the 552 Air Control Wing (flying the E-3 Sentry aircraft, capable of airborne combat management and deep-look surveillance), 3rd Combat Communications Group (air traffic control services throughout the world, wherever the U.S. military is or might be located), the 38th Engineering Installation Group (global responsibility for Air Force communications facilities), the 507th Air Refueling Wing (supporting global U.S. and NATO mid-air refueling and AWACS missions), the Oklahoma Defense Distribution Depot (storage, inspection, issue, inventory, preservation, packaging, pickup and delivery of military stuff), and the Navy's Strategic Communications Wing ONE (communications with ballistic missile submarines).

West of Tinker, high speed freeways—Interstate 35 (Laredo, Texas to Duluth, Minnesota) and I-40 (Barstow, California to Wilmington, North Carolina)—meet, merge, then go their separate ways near the North Canadian River (renamed the Oklahoma River), downtown Oklahoma City buildings clearly visible from the elevated concrete ribbons. East of this inter- section, I-40 passes between Tinker Air Force Base and the Midwest Regional Medical Center where Genevieve lies in the intensive care unit. And along I-40, at all hours of the day, and all days of the week, a steady stream of America exceeds the speed limits, tracking that boundary between an ICU where no effort is spared to maintain an eighty-six-year-old woman's vital signs, on the north, and an establishment whose mission is to deliver weapons of mass destruction anywhere and everywhere in the world, with unparalleled efficiency and speed, on the south.

Afterword

The incongruity of this juxtaposition between Tinker Air Force Base and the Midwest Regional Medical Center could easily be the first brush stroke of some writer's portrait of the United States, an evolving nation, and in a way, validation of historian Angie Debo's claim about the state of Oklahoma, namely, that its history is a compressed version of American history. Debo's assertion, in 1949, was "...all the experiences that went into the making of the nation have been speeded up. Here all the American traits have been intensified." She also took a bolder step, claiming that "the one who can inter- pret Oklahoma can grasp the meaning of America in the modern world."

This juxtaposition between life and death in Oklahoma City also is a reflection of our modern technology, using as example the near-miraculous developments in medicine beside the sophistication of late twentieth-century weaponry. At one extreme, south of Interstate 40, I see a massive profes- sional military establishment deployed globally, far more widespread than armies and navies of either the Roman Empire at the height of its second-century glory, or the nine- teenth-century British Empire at its most extensive.

Aside from sports, my daily news, no matter where it comes from or how it's delivered, is my picture of a powerful nation and the global environment in which it is embedded. This portrait consists largely of death and destruction, religious fanaticism, political posturing, expressions of hatred, conflict, financial troubles or crimes, and the culture wars. In both of the newspapers to which I subscribe, daily pulse letters address, often in derogatory and sarcastic tones, what has become a defining political issue of the American Third Millennium: a woman's right to obtain a safe abortion. From what I read on the editorial pages, expressions of my fellow Americans, it's okay to kill a full-grown Iraqi but not to terminate a pregnancy. On [my] cable television station, an American sniper, interviewed in Baghdad, refers to insurgents as "bad guys." It's okay to kill "bad guys" but not okay to kill innocent embryos. But the subtext in the rest of my newspaper also tells me it is okay to behave—as a nation—in ways that turn innocent embryos into trained killers within a short nineteen years.

At the other extreme, north of Interstate 40, I see an aging human population, sustained by a medical establishment that can only be described as a borderline science fiction manifestation of technology. The administrative species that appeared on August 14, 1935, when Franklin Roosevelt signed the Social Security Act, has now evolved into a financial monster that threatens to bankrupt the nation. Under pressure from the medical community, health care was excluded from Social Security for thirty years until the act was amended in 1965 to provide a form of health insurance—Medicare—for the elderly. Senator Wilbur Mills was successful in adding Medicaid to the amendment, providing health care for the poor regardless of age. This second species also has evolved into a monster, chomping away at state budgets like a ballooning fiscal *Tyrannosaurus rex*. The principles of evolutionary change are at work here as relentlessly as they might be in the world's deserts and tropical forests. If you build something that takes on a life of its own—think Bohemian coffee cake, information technology, and race cars—that "something" will consume the resources that brought it to life.

These are my thoughts during the 800+ miles round trip to and from my childhood home, paying respects to Karen's dying stepmother, reviewing every communication I've ever received from any source about the nature of our universe and the way we humans interact it, all with Angie Debo's assertion ringing in my ears—her claim that Oklahoma is a model for our rapidly evolving nation.

Red Dirt

*Hayes placed the Hedland sand equivalent to a
School Land sand below the Wade sand and above
the Medrano sand ...*

—Louise Jordan, from *Subsurface
Stratigraphic Names of Oklahoma*

Medical records indicate that my aunt Helen probably began having a series of small strokes soon after the death of her dog, Sugar, who, years earlier had followed her home from the post office. Having grown up in a household where stray animals were welcome, Helen took her in, but also checked with local vets and the humane society in an attempt to find Sugar's rightful owner. Nothing came of this effort, so Helen and Sugar became lifelong companions in their small frame house on NW 12th Street in Oklahoma City. Sugar received her name not for being particularly sweet of disposition, but from being snow white except for her nearly black eyes and, of course, after she'd been in the back yard, red stains on her feet and belly from the dirt under Helen's clothesline.

My stepfather, Sam Bristow, shared one trait with Helen, namely, an unyielding kindness toward animals, a kindness that extended to almost any living organism in trouble, and Helen without Sugar was very much in trouble. When Sam found Helen she was dehydrated, unable to get up from her couch and, according to her doctor, within hours of death. We got the telephone call in late June, and within a few days we were once again traversing that blistering signature landscape across Kansas, to a rendezvous with family history in Oklahoma. After the requisite visit to the hospital, we went to Helen's house. Biologists are always biologists; we cannot ever keep from analyzing living organisms, even when they're our own sole-surviving paternal relatives. No matter how elegant, dignified, fastidious, or beloved a human being has been for her first ninety years, when in that ninety-first year her dog dies and she's alone and unable to take care of herself, nature begins to reclaim the premises. The small frame house on NW 12th Street was an entomological disaster.

I wondered what had happened to Sugar's body. Helen was not strong enough to dig a grave through that red clay, but I stepped outside through the kitchen door anyway just to satisfy my curiosity. It was 104° F in the back yard; heat reflected off the garage wall, searing the side of my face. Sugar was nowhere to be found, and there was no mound of freshly turned red dirt, but there among the pieces of a small rock garden, assembled by my aunt from items my grandfather had collected, was a large calcite crystal. Like the dog, this crystal was pure white, except, of course, for red stains on the bottom where it had been in contact with Oklahoma.

Out of curiosity I wander into the back room of Helen's garage. As a child, visiting my grandfather's house at 531 SW 11th, I'd held an almost obsessive fascination with a "back room," essentially an add-on storage shed, whose shadowy contents were barely visible through a window covered with dust and a dirty screen. Helen's back room had a similar character, although with Sugar dead and her mistress in the hospital there are no unspoken taboos about entry, so I push hard on a reluctant door until it swings open, banging against shelves stacked with empty boxes. A squirrel explodes from an open barrel of sunflower seeds, shoots up into the rafters and disappears through a hole somewhere in the roof. Helen had to have her bird feeders; they now hang, empty, from several places in the yard.

I wonder how that barrel of bird and squirrel food came into being in that particular time and place. Helen never learned to drive; she could not have weighed more than a hundred pounds. Someone had to have delivered both the barrel and its contents and put them where enterprising squirrels could follow their noses through some crack, into dark and forbidden territory where was laid out, as free for the taking as if in Squirrel Heaven, more black oil sunflower seeds than any of them could expect to see in one place in a lifetime.

Similarly, but following my curiosity instead of my nose, I start searching for something interesting, something the mental equivalent of seeds. There, at the back of a workbench along the north wall, are rocks—barite crystals, or rose rocks as they are called, almost affectionately, by Oklahomans, fossil clams, a 200-million-year-old rugose coral, a piece of an ammonite. After my grandfather died, Helen sold the house on SW 11th and moved to NW 12th. I'm sure she paid cash for the latter. I have no idea who moved her. Someone had made sure that my grandfather's rocks, or at least a representative sample of them, also made the trip across town.

I put the piece of coral in my pocket. It's one I'd collected from a stream near Weeping Water, Nebraska, and sent to my grandfather decades earlier. He'd promptly cut off the upper end, making several slices, which he then polished until you could see their details—septal patterns by which some pale-ontologist could identify this one, perhaps to species, and fusilinid foraminiferans—amoebas with shells—packed into the coral's gastrovascular cavity. Two hundred million years ago, somewhere in warm shallow seas that would eventually become part of a landlocked, mid-continental Nearctic steppe, the digestive system of a single coral about the size of your thumb became home for hundreds of one-celled ani-mals, each the size and shape of a rice grain. Then 200 million years later, some kid from Oklahoma, wading into a stream, finds this one coral polyp, now a rock, instantly recognizes that rock for what it is, puts it in his pocket, sends it to another kid in Oklahoma, who then cuts it into slices, polishes the cut faces so that you can see an ecological relationship now buried into the depths of time, and glues the slices onto a pair of cufflink blanks ordered from a hobby catalog. Both kids are anything but children; one is a tenured college pro-fessor and the other is retired, even though he never, or at least rarely ever, held a formal job. It's just that that they still act like kids when given any opportunity, especially an oppor-tunity having anything to do with fossils, crystals, or stones. Maybe I should say "acted" instead of "act," because one of them—like Sugar—is dead. I close the garage back room door, pulling hard against the frame. The squirrels can have whatever they want; Helen will never again be in this room.

Back outside in the yard, I take a closer look at the rock garden, reconstructing my grandfather's decisions about what pieces of the landscape to pick up, and Helen's decision about which of those pieces to move, once the house she grew up in was sold. Months later, making sure the place is ready for an estate sale, Karen, my sister Teresa, cousin Ed, and I clean out everything of any potential sentimental value, putting old Christmas cards in boxes, smiling at what Helen had clipped from newspapers in the 1950s, and dividing up the leftovers from Grandpa Frank and Great Grandpa John—straight razors, sharpening stones of exceptional quality, wire-rimmed glasses, books, albums of photographs taken with various box cameras dating back into the early twentieth century—all revealing what these people held to be dear and of lasting value. I could understand the sharpening stones; I could appreciate the decision to buy a new straight razor and put the old one in a drawer, in which it would be discovered a half-century hence.

Among the indicators of personality long gone from Earth, few surpass a thin paperbound booklet entitled *Uranium in Oklahoma*. My grandfather, intrigued by the Cold War but manifesting that intrigue in his own particular way, bought a Geiger counter and went looking for radioactivity. He never found enough to pay for both his travels and his counter, much less to turn Oklahoma into a nuclear arsenal. What he did leave was a report of his travels and dozens of pictures, all of which Helen had faithfully saved, along with some of his rocks. What the Russians had delivered to my family in the 1950s was not a star-tipped missile warhead; it was a legitimate reason to get in your car, drive out in the country, and go dig around in red dirt.

The Russians delivered this reason to simply go exploring as best one could in a part of the world where exploration was a reason for being. Indeed, the very word "exploration" was co-opted by the petroleum industry to the extent that it became synonymous with digging. Out on any two-lane blacktop, passing through isolated towns with small drilling and oil well service companies, you inevitably see chain link fences with pickups, stacks of pipe, sometimes portable rigs, and other large equipment only the initiated know how, or better yet why, to use. The activity in these yards may have waxed and waned with the price of domestic crude, but tires, wheels, and lower door panels are always stained dirt red— just like Sugar and the calcite crystal; contact with the land makes a lasting change in the appearance even of heavy metal.

Along the highway shoulder outside of town, beyond portable drilling rigs waiting for some human's decision on where and when to dig, lie dead skunks, 'possums, and raccoons, casualties of nighttime tavern traffic. Dead skunks' white stripes are always stained red. If you stop and pick up a particularly fresh badger, thinking maybe the skin would make a nice addition to your collection of natural souvenirs, the belly will be stained red. Nothing, it seems, can live in this part of North America without showing evidence of having encountered Permian surface geology—soils laden with iron and derived from a period in Earth's history when oxygen levels were high. My grandfather's car was always dirty; red clay was always packed up under the wheel wells, splattered there along some muddy road where he drove, like every wildcatter of the early oil boom days walking around with his geologist's pick, convinced there lay a financial windfall of indescribable size and importance just beneath the next hill.

The windfall never comes. Instead, we have photographs. A group of men stands on a cut bank beneath a tarp rigged as a tent. To the far right is my grandfather. He's smiling, squinting at the camera. We also have his notes on the back. "First commercial carnotite find at Cement Caddo Co. Found in School gymnasium yard. Sold to Lucius Pitkin Inc. Grants N. Mex. 13 tons ore, averaging 2.66 assay brought $3417.00 and a $2400 bonus by the Atomic Energy commission. Stringer, was 70ft long—averaged less than 3 ft wide and two feet thick. Had the deposit covered an acre, would have brought over $400,000.00. Lister Brothers of Chickasha finders." At the time—middle 1950s—$400,000 would indeed have been a small fortune for these men. Whatever geological vagaries had conspired to deliver this $6000 "70 ft" shallow stringer of carnotite to a schoolyard in southwestern Oklahoma also had conspired to tease this group of explorers with the same mineral bait that had snagged oil boomers a generation earlier and land boomers a generation before that. All six men in the Caddo County photograph could not have been full-time prospectors. Five of them are young enough to need a day job. Only my grandfather looks carefree, standing there in a plaid shirt with his hand on his hip, a man beside a stringer.

I never saw my grandfather get close to a typewriter, so I have no idea who typed *Uranium in Oklahoma*, who actually put on paper what I'm sure my grandfather was thinking about the "first commercial carnotite find" as this picture was taken. Maybe Helen did the secretarial work. The result was quintessentially geologist Oklahoman:

> The reason for this success is the optimism of the American individual not bound by too much orthodox thinking and tradition. Some heretics even found Uranium where it was not supposed to be present.
>
> It took many years to develop the science of petroleum geology to what it is now. Today's current petroleum literature on the technical and practical use of science has gone a long way from the original anticlimal [*sic*] theory, and the carbon ratio of rocks in locating oil fields. We are now about in the same comparative stage in our Uranium thinking as we were back in 1880 in petroleum geology.
>
> Fifty-five years ago the press and stage, and most of the Oklahoma public laughed at the crazy wildcatters. I know, because I was here. When the first reports on the Oklahoma City discovery reached Tulsa it was all a joke, and only propaganda among the smart boys in the hotel lobbies. I know, I was there, and I also remember the Anadarko Basin sneers.
>
> Don't let the fundamentalists laugh you out of court. This generation doesn't know these facts, and the old timers either forgot or are dead. These statements may not make me popular with some individuals, but as I don't expect any reward, I should worry.
>
> If you are looking for ultra sound investments, with a certain profit, buy U.S. Bonds. But if you have some hidden yen for adventure, and feel a little reckless, you can go crazy with

the rest of us ridgerunners. I guarantee you will have fun and maybe so make the first page.

All this impending fun and potential fame rested firmly on yellow, non-fluorescent, rock of a gypsum-like 2 on the hardness scale—thus scratchable with a pocket knife, hardness 5.5, or even a fingernail, hardness 2.5—as opposed to diamonds which are at 10, the max, and therefore scratcher of all lesser minerals. Carnotite is hydrated potassium uranyl vanadate; its chemical formula is $K_2(UO_2)_2(VO_4)_2-1-3H_2O$. It's the "U for Uranium" portion that made the Atomic Energy Commission cough up a $2400 bonus for the small vein in a Caddo County schoolyard, although the "V for Vanadium" is also a militarily important chemical element, being a component of high-strength steel. K is for potassium, an essential participant in the cellular reactions that allow nerve impulses to flow from one's brain to the fingers, or vice versa. O is for oxygen, the most widely recognized vocabulary word in the intellectual domain of chemistry. H is for hydrogen, or Hindenburg; we remember the latter primarily because of the former, which ignited in one of the most spectacular explosions of history, destroying in a few seconds the largest aircraft to ever fly anywhere, along with its passengers and consequently, at least for a short while, the concept of easy and glamorous transatlantic travel. H_2O, of course, is water, the universal solvent and thus the medium in which life on Earth—even human life, if one considers the small fraction of us that is hair, skin, and bone—is suspended. As is the case with all chemical compounds, it's the combination of parentheses, dashes, and subscript numbers that make carnotite carnotite and not something else, in a manner no less determinative than the combination of choices, experiences, associations, and accoutrements made Sugar, the house on NW 12th Street, Helen, my grandfather, their memories, and, of course, their rocks, an essential component of one American family's existence.

A line drawn on Oklahoma from north to south just east of the 99th Meridian starts at about where the Salt Fork of the Arkansas River crosses the Kansas state line northwest of Alva, in Woods County, then proceeds over mostly red Permian-age dirt interrupted by Quaternary alluvial soils that support the cottonwoods and willows marking braided rivers and deeply cut creeks. Paleozoic outcrops lie north of the Ft. Sill Military Reservation and west of Chickasha—named, like so many Oklahoma towns, from a Native American word, in this case perhaps meaning "rebel," or, alternatively a variant of "Chickasaw," one of the "civilized tribes" displaced from the southeastern United States and moved along the Trail of Tears to what is now western Oklahoma.

Ordovician limestones thrust up through hard scrabble farm land north of Cement, right across the Caddo County line, and south of that, an amoeba-shaped bubble of Cambrian igneous formations known as the Wichita Mountains covers much of Comanche County, and therefore much of Ft. Sill. Geronimo is said to have leapt to his death from one of the split faces of such a fire-born rock rather than submit to capture, but that's an Edwards Plateau version of an urban legend. Geronimo actually ended up riding in Teddy Roosevelt's inauguration parade and died of pneumonia at Ft. Sill outside Lawton, Oklahoma. Signal Mountain, upon which generations of new second lieutenants have practiced their cannon fire at abandoned tanks, received its name from messages, sent from its summit and conveyed as smoke columns, between Indian bands.

Packing my grandfather's library—consisting almost entirely of books about the Old West—I can also envision him driving his beat up late '40s model Ford out onto Highway 62 west of Chickasha, Geiger counter on the seat beside him, winding through Anadarko following Highway 9, and living in some kind of a dream world of adventure, exploration, and raw earth, perhaps even involving friendly encounters with Native Americans, all healthy, dignified, and independent, not uprooted and sent packing a thousand miles into a land of cactus and rattlesnakes. Somewhere near Cement he would meet up with the Lister Brothers, scan his detector over the crumbly yellow rocks in the Caddo County school yard, pull out his pocket knife to check the hardness then stand back with his hand on his hip for a photograph. I have no idea how they split up the money. There is no question in my mind that all of these men believed completely, unequivocally, in what they were doing: digging in the red Oklahoma dirt for their fortunes. There was as much dirt under their fingernails as under their fenders, and it was equally embedded, as incapable of being washed away as the stain on a dead skunk's stripe.

The Lister Brothers, if that's indeed who these men were, standing beside Frank Janovy in the photograph, represent one of humanity's few clearly definable relationships with the planet upon which we evolved, a relationship that may, in fact, have shaped much of the Oklahoma personality. The Cambrian period ended approximately 500 million years ago, the Paleozoic era ended about 270 million years later, and conversation fragments heard on Tulsa streets commonly concern these events. Regardless of whatever myths ultraconservative Oklahoma Bible Belt literalists tend to pound into their obedient and unsuspecting children's brains, it is common knowledge even among roughnecks out on a drilling rig south of Durant that since the Paleozoic era ended the Earth's crust has undergone massive reconstruction. Thus the Cambrian granite Wichita Mountains represent a truly ancient reassembly of planetary surface, and the carnotite vein in a nearby Caddo County schoolyard is little more than a lucky— at least for the Lister Brothers—poke through dirt that is itself very likely an assemblage of soils carried hundreds of miles by water and thousands of miles by air to be dropped in the southwest quarter of former Indian Territory.

Few metaphors better describe Earth's crustal turmoil than a serious automobile accident, one that crushes bumpers, doors, grills, fenders, underlying struts and supports, paint, and a driver's future, all into a tangled and unrecognizable mass of metal and color. Few metaphors better describe Oklahomans' approach to this accident than the sculptures of John Chamberlain who, since the late 1950s, has been making an international reputation out of metal debris produced when Detroit's finest collide. Like Chamberlain himself must do in a junkyard, the Lister boys and their self-styled ridgerunner who'd watched those early wildcatters fail and succeed spectacularly, walked out on the North American crustal plate expecting—expecting—to find something of value, deposited there through no fault of their own. And like must be the case with Chamberlain or any other artist who makes his or her pieces from found objects, expectations turn eventually into assumptions that if one looks long enough, one finds. The Lister boys found $6000 worth of uranium ore; Chamberlain finds images that connect with neural networks that in turn send signals to fingers that write big checks so they can take his pieces home.

When looking and finding are our business, and accidents are our raw material, then experience tells us that we do a whole lot more looking than we do finding. Like artists, ridgerunners fail far more often than they succeed. And like artists, this facet of their profession eventually turns into a fact of their life: failure is the price of success and if you're afraid of the former forget the latter. This core characteristic of explorers is in stark contrast to that of the farmer who buys insurance against failure and who therefore represents another of our clearly defined relationships with the planet. The statement that "if you look hard enough you will find" differs significantly from the one that claims "if you work hard enough you will produce" only to the extent that "look" and "work" are separate activities, indeed separate ideas. Thus whatever "work" a person like my grandfather might do, I suspect, is little more than a means to support his or her "looking."

Is this antagonistic but mutualistic relationship between looking and working a hard-wired one? I believe so. I believe that a drive to explore is inherited, and a drive to insure against failure is similarly passed along with one's genes. A "successful" choice of profession is not a choice at all, but is, instead, like a carnotite outcrop in Caddo County, a unique encounter where opportunity collides with nature. Workers dominate a population, physically, mentally, and politically when there is no opportunity to go exploring. But when looking becomes legitimate work, then explorers rule the cultural landscape. With the first discovery that valuable minerals lie beneath the terrain, explorers assume their cultural dominance. When successful exploration becomes commonplace, then the nobility of pure exploration turns into entitlement. My claim is that this last rule is universal, obeyed not only by men sitting in Tulsa offices, but by men half a world away in flowing robes.

What separates present-day Oklahoma from present-day Saudi Arabia is not the probability of finding oil, but the probability of failure to find oil provided one digs in the dirt. When failure is likely—somewhat akin to that of trying to write a successful novel or make an acclaimed work of art—only the driven retain enough hope to in turn sustain nobility equivalent to that of the Lister Brothers squinting into a camera beside their carnotite vein. When the chance of failure is slim or none, explorers devolve into shoppers and pay for their sprees with their nobility. These are simple lessons from the heart of America for an evolving nation peering into its future. Oh, but there is an additional simple lesson for evolving nations, a lesson that also sprouts, unwanted but acknowledged, sort of like weeds: minerals do not multiply like corn. You don't produce oil. You find oil. There is only one category of natural resource that multiplies if given a chance, yet must be "harvested" by exploration, and that is wild things: microbes, fungi, plants, and animals. And of this last type of natural resource, Oklahoma has an abundance. Had the Lister boys been looking for birds, they'd have found a bunch.

About the same time my grandfather decided to go prospecting for uranium, another individual came to Oklahoma from back East because of the geology. This one had already had a career of fun and had "maybeso made the first page," although in this case the page was that of books and arcane ornithological journals and the fun was that to be had only by a professional golfer or birdwatcher. This one was a birdwatcher.

Why would a world-famous scientist, one who had made his reputation through study of birds in the Arctic and Mexico, decide that Oklahoma was the place to finish a career, to write his definitive book? When asked, ornithologist George Miksch Sutton would reply something to the effect that the Rocky Mountain uplift extended down into the Panhandle; Harmon, Jackson, and Tillman counties in the southwest corner represented the northern extremes of the Edwards Plateau; the

Eastern Deciduous Forest lapped over the northeastern quarter of the state; the Southeastern Oak/Pine Forest occupied much of the area between Stringtown, Darwin, Lutie, and Arkansas; and U.S. Highway 77 marked the boundary between tall- and shortgrass prairie.

Poking up through this amalgamation were a dozen mountain ranges with names like Arbuckle, Wichita, and Kiamichi, none of which would qualify as real mountains to anyone from Vermont or Colorado, but which nevertheless were faithfully labeled as such on maps and equally faithfully accepted as such by anyone who knew their half-a-billion-year history. Sutton then left it to you to supply the birdy details. Instead of talking about plants and geological features he could just as easily have said "magpie, road runner, grasshopper sparrow, and red-cockaded woodpecker." Anyone who knew birds could then have drawn the surface geology maps, vegetation maps, and isometric lines of annual precipitation. And if you called the Arbuckles "mountains" in dead seriousness, you could easily supply the subsurface topography, but instead of magpies you'd be talking about shales, dolomites and isoclines.

Of course by the time I encountered Sutton, common geological terms such as *Arbuckle, dolomite, gypsum, shale,* and a million others that local grownups seemed to toss about with such knowing abandon were very familiar words. I may not have had a clue what they meant—except for *gypsum,* a very large, soft and crumbling sample of which was behind our garage—but I'd heard them repeatedly for years. I knew certain kinds of people used these words over and over again, and that such individuals used them in both casual conversation with their friends and in serious business conversations immediately after which decisions involving thousands, if not tens of thousands, of dollars would then be made and spent.

The conversations themselves were not entirely lost on my young mind. I learned how to make a long distance telephone call from listening to my father ask questions about sands with names, about tracings on electric logs, then hang up, pack a small bag, softly tell my mother something about when he'd be back, then take off in the middle of the night for a drilling rig wreaking physical havoc on blackjack oak woodland a hundred miles down some muddy road. From those conversations, I also learned that when your business is that of exploring the natural world, then "9" and "5" are data points, not hours of obligation to some system constructed by human beings. That our lives were inextricably intertwined with a natural universe over which we had no control was a given. It was also a given that the lives of everyone I knew were also equally intertwined. Small wonder Oklahomans collected rocks and hung bird feeders for the squirrels.

Once in a while my father would take me to the field. Most of the time it must have been summer, although I distinctly remember being taken out of school one day to attend an "Oil Show" in Tulsa. There in a gigantic exhibition hall were shiny new versions of the filthy, greasy, red splattered, machines I'd seen men use to dig thousands of feet into Oklahoma dirt. I picked up souvenirs, literature, and a yardstick. The company names on these items were household words—Halliburton, Schlumberger—the former euphonic enough to say it often just to feel the "l's" roll off your tongue, the latter—"*schlum-ber-jay*"—my first lesson in French. I didn't know what these industrial behemoths did, exactly, but I knew that when certain tasks needed to be done out in the field, someone would call them. "Halliburton" seemed to be synonymous with drilling mud; "Schlumberger" seemed to have the monopoly on electric logs.

Every Oklahoma kid knew what drilling mud and electric logs were for. "Mud" was, and for that matter still is, an intricately concocted soup used to lubricate a drill bit and carry up grindings, or "samples." Electric logs were for occupying fathers. Late into the evening, cigarette smoke curling up onto the ceiling, my father studied various ink tracings on strips of paper laid out on the dining room table over large maps. When he found the patterns he was looking for, he'd either make tiny circles marks on the maps or pack his stuff and go to the field. When he came back, our garage floor would be covered with little cloth bags, each containing what looked and felt like fine, sharp, gravel. Each bag would be carefully tagged and laid out in sequence. In daily conversation the word *samples* had an Oklahoma meaning: a handful of rock chips through which you could see a hundred million years into the past.

When summer arrived, and I got to go along out to an oil well, my father would stop and collect fossils. I learned the word *brachiopod* on one such trip, and have never forgotten the telltale signs of "brachs" in limestone, or, for that matter, in the marble tops of fine furniture. One saw planetary history in curving lines. One learned to see Earth in terms of its organisms and their natural products. As a senior in college, wondering what to do with a degree in mathematics, I enrolled in George Sutton's ornithology class. It may seem a stretch, but at the time birds and their nests didn't seem that much different from Mesozoic vegetation and oil, or, for that matter, carnotite. All were distributed in accordance with certain landscapes, whether these were laid out on the surface or a mile below the ground, and the links between surface and subsurface were never questioned by anyone—adults or their children—with whom I interacted. The fundamental rules about one's relationships with nature had been established by the cultural milieu of Oklahoma: first, you studied landscape; second, you assumed that landscape could tell you something about its history and its contents; third, no matter whether you were looking for oil or birds, you went into that landscape—physically and literally—as a way of life.

Sutton's classes were always small, usually small enough so that we could all fit into his green, 1952, three-hole Buick. There were no seat belts in 1952 Buicks. Ornithologists drive at highway speeds, but they also watch birds continually. If you fear for your physical safety, never get in a car with an ornithologist. If you have a fear of growing up ignorant of natural history, always get in a car with an ornithologist. George Sutton came to Oklahoma to write a book, eventually published in 1967 by the University of Oklahoma Press and entitled, of course, *Oklahoma Birds*. The subtitle is *Their Ecology and Distribution, with Comments on the Avifauna of the Southern Great Plains*. The dust jacket illustration is a watercolor portrait of a Harlan's hawk, painted by Sutton. Scattered throughout are pen-and-ink drawings: roadrunner with a limp *Cnemidophorus sexlineatus* hanging from its beak, an osprey in the act of alighting on a dead limb, two shovelers making a "V" of ripples on a shallow glassy pond, a loggerhead shrike gripping a thorny branch.

All of these drawings have an inherent narrative. A roadrunner could catch one of the fastest and most wily lizards ever to evolve. A shrike would choose a branch with thorns because shrikes stick their prey on thorns, a sort of larder, for later consumption. On page 90 of Oklahoma Birds there is a statement regarding turkey vultures: "On Salt Plains National Wildlife Refuge, Alfalfa County, pair nested each summer 1954–1965 in tumble-down shed." The phraseology is telegraphic, typical of systematic work in biological sciences. Inside the front cover there is another statement regarding turkey vultures, this one in India ink, in Sutton's handwriting: "Inscribed to my friend John Janovy, Jr., who will, perhaps remember the baby buzzards in the old shack on the Salt Plains refuge whenever he uses this book! George Miksch (Doc) Sutton Norman, Oklahoma February 9, 1968." I remembered the baby buzzards well. Crawling into the dim shadows through a hole in the boards, I'd come face to face with a turkey vulture chick old enough to stand, thrust its beak out to within a few inches of my nose, and slowly regurgitate an unbelievably rotten smelling mass of half-digested road kill rabbit. Whatever desire I had to interact with adolescent vultures disappeared at that moment. Describing this event, now forty-plus years in the past, the memory of that smell makes my stomach wrench.

Wherever he went, Sutton carried a shotgun. And wherever my father went, he carried sample bags. When Sutton needed evidence—irrefutable tangible evidence—of what the geological collision had attracted to Oklahoma, or allowed to flourish there, he would raise his shotgun and collect a sample. When my father needed evidence—irrefutable tangible evidence—of what the geological collision had distributed far beneath his feet, he stood by a mud trough at the slush pit and collected rock chips, washed them, bagged them, tagged them, and took them back to a cheap motel room, or sometimes a trailer beside a rig, and studied them under a microscope. Sutton's tools consisted of scissors, forceps, sticks, cotton batting, corn meal, borax, carbon tetrachloride, needles, thread, pins, and cardboard. My father's tools consisted of forceps, small metal trays of exactly the right shape so that rock chip samples could be easily returned to their bag, and a set of beautifully sharpened colored pencils. Sutton's products were bird skins—warblers, vireos, wrens, sandpipers—beautifully prepared and preened, carefully labeled with standard tags tied to their crossed feet, and placed in a white steel case with flat wooden drawers and a small box for dichloride crystals to discourage insects. My father's products were maps—locations and topography of particular, and often cryptically named, shales and sands far below the ground—and decisions—keep drilling or set casing. Sutton also produced maps, in this case distributions of nesting species, locations where each species had been sighted, all linked back to a database with dates—a space-time continuum of moving animals.

Sutton's database consisted of small loose-leaf notebooks. One section was a daily chronicle of events—where he went, who he was with, weather conditions, observations on habitat. The other section was a species list. Each species had its own pages, with chronological entries. Most of this material was typed on a manual typewriter with carbon ribbon. Handwritten entries were in permanent India ink. Sutton's notebooks would last as long as the Dead Sea Scrolls. Nowadays, this information would be put into computer files, and would be called a "relational database." Assuming there is no nuclear holocaust in the next thousand years, assuming that museum and library archivists do their work for a millennium, assuming our institutions still exist, then a doctoral student writing her thesis on the history of ornithology will be able to put on a pair of white gloves, open those Sutton notebooks, turn the brittle pages, and read his handwritten notes as clearly as any art historian can read a Rembrandt drawing. The relational database, however, will be gone, gone into the same technological hell where lies every spreadsheet, every unpublished novel, every committee report, every e-mail not printed out on acid-free paper and preserved in archive-quality folders away from sunlight and every hard drive not confiscated by the Federal Bureau of Investigation.

As a nation, we've produced ephemerality; as an individual, Sutton produced a permanent and personal vision of the world as it existed in Oklahoma for a thirty-five-year period. As an individual, my father produced a personal and permanent vision of the Earth as it existed in what we now call "Oklahoma" for a 400-million-year period. My father's maps were large, made of some kind of high quality drawing cloth. Sutton's "maps" were notebook paper. Both men had a lifetime's worth of these constructions, snapshots of the planet as viewed from within their professions and moments of time frozen forever in the products of their hands and minds. Sutton made us keep such notebooks for his courses in ornithology. My own entry for October 15, 1960, reads:

> Oct 15—Tishamingo [sic] hatchery, Regan, Okla.—We left Dr. Sutton's house a little after 6:00 AM and drove first to the hatchery a little way south of Sulphur. The temp was in the high 50s and the sky was mostly overcast and the wind was from the NE at about 5–10mph. We took a short walk down past the shed to the brushy area but didn't go in, saving it for later. We turned back and started circling the ponds. The group split in half and went around the first and largest and then we all split up and walk among the smaller ponds. As usual on our trips the tall grass was very wet and we were completely soaked after a few minutes. After walking over the ponds we went back and started thru the brush north of the shed. After scouring the brush we headed out across the pasture, walking north until we crossed the road and went thru some open brush until we got to Lowrant Lake, very clean and clear water, about an acre or more. After surveying the lake we turned back to the woods, walked along Buckhorn creek, back across the road, and finally into the grassy xxxxx west of the brush north of the hatchery. After walking xx that area we returned to the car and drove to the Tishamingo [sic] hatchery at Regan, Okla. By this time the sky had cleared off and the weather had warmed up quite a bit. After a short delay while Dr. Sutton located the manager we walked thru the ponds in much the same manner as at the other pond. It

was well after noon by this time so we drove to the Buckhorn café at Davis, had a good lunch, and returned home.

And what did we see on this expedition?

Downy woodpecker <u>Dendrocopus pubescens</u> (Linnaeus) Oct 15—Regan trip—One flew out of tree in the open brush near Lowrant lake.

Horned Lark <u>Eremophila alpestris</u> (Linnaeus) Oct 15—Regan trip—One came flying over us as we were standing near the ponds at the Sulphur hatchery.

The bird list for this trip could go on for many pages. The downy woodpecker page has entries from January 31, 1959, to December 3, 1960, from the woods along the South Canadian River near Norman to a place called Hog Creek. The horned lark page has entries from February 7, 1959, to November 26, 1960, from a place called Indian Springs to the highlands near Boise City in the northwest corner of the panhandle. The typing is in two different fonts, one of which—Elite—I recognize as the portable manual Karen received as a high school graduation present, a 1958 version of a laptop. The other font is Pica; whatever machine it was produced on has long since disappeared from both my possession and my memory. Could I find those bird-watching sites again? Probably not, except for the Tishomingo fish hatchery. Nowadays we'd carry a GPS unit and our notebooks would contain latitudes and longitudes down to the thousandths of a degree. Forty or fifty years hence we would be able to return to the exact same spot where we'd seen a downy woodpecker fly "out of tree in the open brush near Lowrant lake," look around, and determine exactly what that small piece of America had become during the preceding half-century.

Would there still be downy woodpeckers in the open brush near Lowrant Lake? Probably; Lowrant Lake is not in a place suitable for a Wal Mart Superstore. Would you still be able to hire some actors, dress them in period garb for a group portrait underneath a tarp beside that same carnotite vein in a dusty Caddo County schoolyard? Probably so; Caddo County evolves rather slowly these days. But can you hire another George Miksch Sutton at the University of Oklahoma? No. No academic institution of any size in the United States of

America would hire someone who collects birds with a shotgun for evidence of who lived where when then writes books about the geographical and temporal distribution of those same birds, all the while keeping daily notes and drawing pictures in India ink. American academic institutions want the same thing American professional basketball players want: money and respect, but respect of the kind afforded winners and massive belligerent armies, not the kind engendered by white-haired college professors taking students out to places where they can come face to face with a vomiting vulture chick.

A more intriguing question is whether a thousand years hence downy woodpeckers will still be flying out of the brush near Lowrant Lake. History tells us that if museums and libraries do their work and we are still a civilized, semi-literate and semi-solvent nation, then Sutton's watercolors, my father's maps, and my own class notes from 1960 are more likely to be here a millennium hence than are downy woodpeckers. Even in Oklahoma one can find medieval art, portraits of Madonna and Child. Even in Oklahoma, evidence can be found, among the objects hidden away in private homes as well as in museums, for what the world was like a thousand years ago. And even in Oklahoma, as in every other state of our nation, there is plenty of evidence for what the world will be like in another thousand years.

The population of Oklahoma City was 204,424 people in 1940, 243,504 in 1950, 365,916 in 1975, and is estimated at 519,034 today. At this rate, Oklahoma City's population doubles every half-century, so that a millennium from now, it will stand at 2.72×10^{11} or 272,000,000,000, or 272 *billion* Okies, almost thirty times the estimated carrying capacity of planet Earth, all dressed in red and heading out for a football game in Norman. The history written in limestone beneath Oklahoma red dirt tells us exactly what will happen if the evolutionary forces at work today continue to work. Brachiopods my father plucked from folded sediments are better predictors of the future than a stockbroker in that gleaming high rise at 210 North Robinson. Thus accumulate the life lessons about what Oklahoma men found when they dug into red dirt, studied rock formations a mile beneath their feet, took their boys along for the ride, and told them what they were seeing.

Afterword

This piece was originally conceived as part of an "Oklahoma book" I've been thinking about and working on for years. It is an attempt to express that part of a family relationship in which a father involves his children in his business, not necessarily on purpose, at least all the time, but more or less as default behavior. When your dad's a geologist, and your grandfather likes rocks and practices being a serious amateur geologist, then you grow up talking about Earth in some rather characteristic ways. You notice the color of dirt; you notice the layered sedimentary formations revealed by a road cut; you study stone floors and stair cases as you walk through government buildings; and, you're not afraid to think in terms of plate tectonics and the erosion of mountain ranges. It may seem to be a stretch, but I honestly believe that time spent in the company of applied scientists, namely, my father and his friends, primed me for life as a biologist, and indeed, was the key factor in my decision to become an ornithologist the last semester of my senior year at the University of Oklahoma, two months away from receiving a degree in mathematics.

That decision led me and my family at the time—Karen, my wife; Cynthia Anne, age three, and Jenifer Lynn, age eight months—to UNL. We had no idea what to expect, other than, for the first time, a regular paycheck. What we found was rich opportunity, excellent friends, and magnificent museums, including the Sheldon Museum of Art where Karen has built a successful career as Education Coordinator, deeply respected by all who truly understand her contributions. Our son, John III, was born in Lincoln and eventually returned to a successful career in real estate. But my biggest surprise, completely unexpected, was the thousands of excellent, challenging, and interesting young people who walk into the University of Nebraska every August. The next three chapters, in Part II—Aksarben Spelled Backward, deal with the past forty-three years on the faculty at UNL, with much of the focus being on the interactions with these students.

PART II

Aksarben Spelled Backward

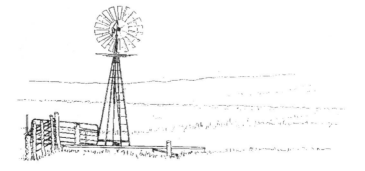

STILL LIFE W MICROSCOPE & JAR

Through a Lens

*But what's to come of it? Nothing, as far as I know:
because most students go there to make money out of
science, or to get a reputation in the learned world.
But in lens-grinding, and discovering things hidden
from our sight, these count for naught. And I am
satisfied too that not one man in a thousand is
capable of such study ... And over and above all, most
men are not curious to know: nay, some even make
no bones about saying, What does it matter whether
we know this or not?*

> —Antony van Leeuwenhoek, 1715,
> in a letter to Gottfried Leibniz
> explaining why he is not training
> people to grind lenses

One year I went to the funeral of a friend who lived in a small town three hundred miles away. The drive out was on a rare, relatively warm and still, February day. I left at 6:00 AM and headed west, and as the sun rose behind me, casting orange light into my rear-view mirrors, large clouds of waterfowl, mainly snow geese, drifted over the corn stubble. The small lakes along the interstate had thawed, and their mirror-like surfaces reflected stands of bare trees along their shores, making intriguing visual images that I soon felt compelled to photograph. Fortunately the stillness remained through most of the afternoon, and I eventually got to a place where it was safe to park, retrieve my small digital camera, and take the photographs that had been in my mind for the previous four hours. Then I went to the service; Karen would have gone but she was in California at a professional meeting, so I was alone.

As we gathered in the church hallway, I struck up a conversation with a young gentleman and ended up sitting next to him in the sanctuary. He had started college as a vocal music major, and when we got to the hymns, it was obvious that I was seated next to an individual with a rather incredible voice. And as I listened to this elegant vocal music being delivered into my right ear, appreciating the concert—consisting of a deeply religious hymn, soon to be followed by an even more deeply religious eulogy—I was reminded, strangely, of an assertion by one of the world's most belligerently atheistic biologists, Sir Richard Dawkins: scientists see things that the general public does not, and cannot, see. In this sense, I thought at the time, scientists are quite like opera stars, artists, and soldiers. Indeed, all professionals have experiences that amateurs simply cannot have, and those experiences are their metaphorical "visions."

Most of my visions, as a professional biologist, have been literal ones through a lens, a real, glass, lens, the first, and most addictive of which I was given one time by my father, along with a handful of grass, a quart jar, some water. The lenses were in a little microscope he had played with as a child. I have no idea why he did this act, but it may have been something that someone in his childhood had done: take a bunch of dead grass, put it in a jar with water, put the whole mess in a fairly warm place, and wait two weeks. He had some slides and cover glasses, and who knows where those came from, but one day we put a drop of water on a slide, added a cover glass, and slipped the slide into this little brass microscope. The jar was swarming with *Paramecium*. I was hooked. The microscope became mine. I picked up everything I could find and put it under that lens, just as Antony van Leeuwenhoek had done 250 years earlier, in the process discovering protozoa. Virtually every day after seeing those first paramecia, I studied the surrounding world at a very tiny scale—for entertainment driven by curiosity, the same reasons that sustained van Leeuwenhoek. And, I have been doing this looking through lenses, usually at microscopic things, now for about sixty years.

In addition to their toys—mainly guns, fishing tackle, and geologist's picks—both my father John and grandfather Frank had real microscopes, which they used in their business, although in my grandfather's case, it was very difficult to say he had any real business other than doing just what the hell he wanted to do when he wanted to do it. He never went to college. His earliest memories were of getting beaten up by local boys on the streets of Newark, New Jersey, to where his own father, another John Janovy, had immigrated. Local toughs didn't care for the clothes little Frank wore, which may well have been dresses, or something that looked enough like a dress to warrant a fight. Eventually Frank got on a train going west, disembarking at the old stone railroad station in Beatrice, Nebraska, from where he somehow made his way to Keya Paha County, on the South Dakota border, to be a cowboy. There is no evidence from family records that he had ever touched a horse before stepping off that train in Beatrice.

Nobody knows how Frank made it to Oklahoma City and ended up as a policeman, either, but he did, and married another Bohemian, Anna Vodiska, who bore him four children before dying young. Some time during these years he tried farming, in Cleveland County, Oklahoma, where his only son John, my father with the toy microscope, was born. Eventually the family returned to Oklahoma City, settling in at 531 Maple Street, which later became SW 11th. From there, the four children: Lillian, Helen, John, and Marie, walked to Riverside School. Then, with absolutely no formal training in geology, Frank became a geologist, just like he'd become a cowboy, a cop, and a farmer earlier, and went to work for a fellow Bohemian named Fred Ptak, an attorney who dabbled in oil.

This decision to become a geologist came in the middle of Oklahoma's oil boom. The blackjack scrub around Drumright and Cushing was bubbling with crude, attracting wildcatters and a service industry that included construction crews, drillers, mechanics, cooks, tailors, bankers, and every other kind of opportunistic parasite that flocks to money. Oil, the source of all that money, comes from rocks, and not all rocks, but only certain kinds of rocks. So a man who decided to become a geologist needed a microscope in addition to his hand lens, pocket knife, and instincts, the latter honed by an apprenticeship only another geologist could provide, an informal lesson spent looking at rocks and picking up visual cues to the meaning of words like *shale, schist,* and *dolomite.* Thus Frank acquired a microscope, not one like I'd used to see my first *Paramecium,* the one that used transmitted light, but what we would call today a dissecting microscope, through which you could study rock chips dredged up from the bottom of some Oklahoma hole two thousand feet deep. He also learned enough geology to be useful to drillers, although I have no idea how he did it and never thought to ask before he died. It would not have surprised me very much to discover that he just "picked it up," but from where, or whom, nobody knows. He had some surveying equipment, too, a nice compass, for example, that I now own, along with the dissecting scope and his geologist's pick that probably still has some radioactive carnotite on it.

Nowadays I look through that same dissecting microscope periodically, a century after it was built. It's a Leitz, so it still works well. Through those lenses you can see the crystal-like details in a tiny chip of limestone, see the makeup of a piece of granite and from that makeup estimate the speed with which it cooled after being in a molten state, or you can shine an ultraviolet light on bits of shale and see the yellow glow that means oil. Then you can walk out on the street, where there are people moving about, going shopping, killing time, looking for a job, heading down to the YMCA for their noon workout, all those things that normal people do when they're out on the street, and you can bet the family farm that not one in ten thousand of them can tell you what the surface of a tiny limestone chip looks like under a century-old dissecting microscope.

Nor can one in ten thousand tell you, as they get to the parking garage and start their car, what oil-soaked shale looks like when you shine UV light on it. And if you asked them what they're buying their children for Christmas or birthday, the answer is likely to be electronics, a video game, a metaphorical lens, instead of a real glass one. Through that electronic "lens" these children will see what another human has concocted from timeless stories of conflict and attraction, often chases and shootings and bedroom scenes, not what has been wrought by the collision of their planet's crustal plates.

Instead of showing them something wondrous, mysterious, captivating, about their planet, this electronic lens will separate them from the dirt beneath their feet.

There were, lying around our home in Oklahoma City, other lenses. My father regularly took photographs, using a Rolleiflex, with my sister and me as subjects squinting into the sun. This obvious documentation of family history never happened without me wondering what he was seeing in the view finder. When I finally got a camera of my own one Christmas, a small simplified Rolleiflex knockoff Kodak that used 620 mm roll film, I immediately discovered what you could see through that lens and mirror. You saw your sister, the muskrat hides you'd stretched out on bent coat hangers, your best friend with his shotgun and some ducks he'd killed, your dog, and everything else that was assembled into your life and times. The shutter release was there to capture this record, a sixtieth of a second in some teenager's experience on Earth, a record established by what this kid *saw* through a lens and what he *chose* to capture using that lens and the mechanisms surrounding it. The vision and the choice, I learned early on, were critical factors in the lives of people who look at the world through glass lenses.

In retrospect, such photographs are assumed to tell us what happened. In fact, they tell us what we chose to have happen in the eyes of people who will look at them years hence. So it's a small wonder that once I acquired this power to catch an instant of personal history, I began plotting ways to enhance it. Thus I started casting eyes on my father's other wondrous toy, an Argus C3 that used 35mm film, with which I could stop motion simply by turning a little wheel to 1/300th of a second, but was soon diverted by the discovery of a pair of binoculars stuck away in his closet. As with the microscopes, I had no idea where these lenses came from, but they found a home in my room, from whose windows I carefully studied the lights on distant radio towers, license plates on two Hudsons parked in our neighbors' driveway across a vacant lot, and the front doors of West Nichols Hills Elementary School two blocks away. The doors were especially metaphorical: you could see in the distance where you would be going the next morning, and you knew in advance what was likely to happen in there: reading, writing, and music.

Hunting came later, along with shotguns. At daybreak I sit along the icy shores of Lake Hefner, in a blind constructed of brush, studying—through these binoculars—a line of dark dots making its way through the early morning air a mile away. In so doing I developed another lifelong habit, one that enriches the lives of countless thousands, namely, watching birds, simply watching them, not necessarily studying them, but just watching, answering a simple question: what species are those? "What species are those?" is, it turns out, the most pervasive and enduring biological question of our time, especially if phrased in a more general way—"What is it?"

Later, in the chapter entitled "The Firm," I raise the issue of scientific reputation and the kinds of publications that produce it. This issue is discussed repeatedly throughout the coffee shops and watering holes surrounding American institutions of higher education. How do you get published in *Science* or *Nature*, my students often ask, rhetorically. I know their response; it's a kind of sarcasm only deep knowledge of the nature of science can produce. Such sarcasm is surprisingly insightful, coming from people whose careers have barely started, much less progressed to the jaundiced old professor stage. Their answer, however, stems from early experience of looking through lenses trying to answer biologists' most pervasive and enduring question while constantly hearing behind them a conversation about reputation, grant money, and competitiveness. So how do you get published in *Science* or *Nature?* Discover a new fossil, one of these young scientists will say, with his or her unexpected dose of cynicism, and not just any fossil, but one that tells us something about ourselves.

Picture this scene somewhere in desolate, baked, sub-Saharan Africa. A narrow ribbon of green cuts almost directly north and south through barren outcrops; a shallow stream from distant snowcapped mountains meanders slowly through the valley; a group of men, scattered along the bluffs, sit digging in the clay and chipping away at overlying rocks. The only things they've brought to Ethiopia are their expertise, picks, shovels, some dissecting tools, and, of course, lenses. One yells at the others. They gather around the man who called out, a couple of them stumbling across uneven ground, to look at small pieces laid out in his hand. Teeth. Everyone knows these little rocks are teeth. Everyone does what long ago became a reflex action for all men of their profession: they take hand lenses out of their shirt pockets, pass the fossil teeth around, and put them close up to their eyes, in focus.

The lenses are tethered, each man's hanging from a cord, resting in his pocket until needed. Such hand lenses are more than a fashion statement; they are a paleontologist's badge. On this particular morning these men are seeing their publication in *Science* and they know it. The physical act of putting a lens between their eye and a fossil tooth unleashes a flood of argot in their minds: M_1, M_2, *hypoconulid, entoconid, paraconid*. The molars, from a child's lower jaw, are nearly four and a half million years old. The most enduring and pervasive question—"What is it?"—will be answered in a way that sheds light on the history of *Homo sapiens*, Earth's most narcissistic species, and the only one that we absolutely know for sure is obsessed with its own origins.

What do these men see through their pieces of curved glass? They see shapes—ridges, valleys, tiny versions of the landscape where they sit, but with characteristic forms they recognize as distinct from the tiny valleys and ridges on teeth described by others looking for pieces of our history. This is probably a new species, one of them says. Before their jaunt to Ethiopia is finished, they'll pick up more teeth, and some bones—a piece of lower jaw, an upper arm—from a dozen or more individuals. Depending on what was seen through those lenses, the men may well have said: that's an ape, or that's a human. Instead, the microscopic landscape falls somewhere in between, with characteristics of both. Someone in that group of hot, dusty, and now excited men already sees a published photograph of this four-million-year-old child's tooth. Music plays in his head. It's Dr. Hook's masterpiece, "Cover of the *Rolling Stone*." The man imagines himself buying five copies of *Science*, the tooth in his hand on the cover, then mailing one off to his mother.

I've never been to Ethiopia or held an *Ardipithecus ramidus* tooth in my hand, but I have re-enacted this kind of scene so many times in the past six decades that I'm convinced its description, including the thoughts about music, is fairly accurate. Well, maybe the bit about *Rolling Stone* is a stretch that comes from hanging out with too many young people, but the hand lens in a shirt pocket image is right on target. At home I look around my office and see lens after lens: my own Argus C3, a bunch of Pentaxes—an old Spotmatic, its light meter worn out, a newer and near useless ME-Super, a K-1000 body bought after I went back to simple mechanics and not so simple telephotos and wide angles—a 35mm real film Nikon point and shoot, two Nikon digitals, an Olympus digital, a Sony camcorder, a Sony Mavica digital, several pairs of binoculars, a spotting scope, my grandfather's dissecting scope, my father's dissecting scope, and his Rolleiflex, his Practica SLR, a box of adapters, extension tubes, and 2X converters, a large circular reading glass, a smaller, rectangular reading glass, a $20 pair of reading glasses, and a plastic lens salvaged from a worn-out slide viewer. A very special hand lens, found in my father's office after he died, resides down in the pocket of a camera bag. The cover is black plastic; two lenses, of different magnifications, slide in and out of this cover. As a child I assumed that this wonderful piece of equipment was standard for geologists. As an adult I know the assumption is correct.

Karen calls this stuff "toys." I cannot envision a day that I would not spend looking through one or more lenses, with magnifications ranging from 10× to 1000×, at something biological, starting at daybreak and ending well after dark. Most people consider squirrels to be a nuisance; I consider them essential yard ornaments for study—through lenses. Binoculars sit ready beside the kitchen coffee pot, ready to grab for a quick look at some rodent doing what rodents do all the time: sit, with wind fluffing hair, eating a seed. Later in the morning I unlock my office door at the university and say hello all the familiar faces: Nikon Alphaphot compound microscope fitted with a video camera, a Meiji dissecting scope with camera tube, an American Optical Microstar with trinocular head, a Wild phase-contrast with 10×, 20×, 40×, and 100× objectives and a trinocular head, a Nikon digital Coolpix with special microscope adapter, a Canon Powershot with special microscope adapter, a drawer full of microscope objectives and eye pieces, an ancient Kodak 2×2 carousel slide projector, an Optima digital projector with zoom lens, large reading magnifiers, and all the thousands of specimens that have been studied using this equipment then talked about incessantly.

A student walks in. We're having an argument, he says, about what that bird is out on the stadium. I think it's a falcon, he continues; Gabe thinks it's a pigeon. I look out the window; sure enough, there's a bird perched on the top railing of Memorial Stadium's south end zone. Gabe Langford, a doctoral student whose lab is next door, comes in to argue his point. Surely there are some binoculars around here, I say, and start looking. Of all the lenses in that laboratory, there are no binoculars. I can't believe it. The bird flies; from its body proportions and wing movements, it's obviously a pigeon. This morning the most pervasive and enduring biological question of our time—"What is it?"—gets answered satisfactorily without a lens: *Columba livia*, the European rock dove, invasive throughout the world, bred to delightful diversity on purpose, used by Charles Darwin to demonstrate the process of selection, used by various armies as messengers, surviving beautifully in America's cityscapes, and sitting, frequently, on that sacred monument known as Memorial Stadium. The next day I bring some binoculars to school.

My lab is on the top floor of a building whose architectural style is best described as Lowest Bidder Utilitarian, the same general design one might find in a prison. If you're lucky enough to have a window in such a building, and lucky enough to have wildlife outside, then you need some lenses, not just ones through which you can see the insides of a *Paramecium*, but some that you can use to check out the birds on the stadium. That architectural wonder also provides a cubist composition, like a painting out the window, to break the monotony of sorting papers into piles: quizzes to be graded, memos to be ignored, letters of recommendation to write, and old literature to file away, probably to see the light again only at the end of a career, when there are only two stacks: archives and recycled. But you never know when you're going to need some of this old paper, with a discovery suddenly important for some reason only a scientist would have, so we collect a lifetime's supply. Turning away from the stadium out the window, I see file cabinets full of this stuff, all photocopied using some combination of lenses down in a machine that forces you to adapt to its peculiarities, learning which buttons to push almost like some metaphorical mystery woman. But the bird on the stadium will be no mystery next time; we now have some binocs in the lab.

Somewhere I read the following factoid: the average size of an animal on Earth is about half an inch, one centimeter or so. Personal experiences validate the claim, but none so effectively as a piece of offshore California that shows up in my lab annually on schedule. One fall Monday, every year, a man in Monterey puts an enormous chunk of kelp holdfast in a heavy plastic bag, pours in a bunch of Pacific Ocean water, wires the bag shut, then puts it in another bag, which he also closes, twisting the open end, bending it back on itself, and wrapping it tightly with wire. Then he puts the whole mess in a Styrofoam cooler, throws in a dozen or two frozen gel pacs, lifts the cooler into a cardboard box, tapes the box shut, and calls FedEx. Within twenty four hours, this package arrives at my office door, leaking salt water and smelling like the most wonderful memories—awakening on the beach at Guerrero Negro, awakening on the beach at San Quintin, awakening on the beach at Bahia de Los Angeles.

Kelp, the algal seaweed, makes a tangled matt of tough, branching, thick, fibers on the ocean floor. This matt, the holdfast, anchors the long stipes ("stems") and blades ("leaves"), the latter usually with gas-filled bladders, or pneumatocysts, that function to keep the blades afloat. For a kid in Nebraska, kelp holdfast cannot be described in words; it simply has to be experienced through a lens. On Tuesday morning, the box from Monterey arrives, dripping, delivered to my office door by a stock room employee. I sign for the shipment. Over in the teaching lab, I pull out a razor blade and start slicing through layers of packing tape. Inside is enough wonder to keep a seventy-year-old child busy for days, perhaps weeks, although "busy" is, like beauty, in the mind of the beholder. With kelp holdfast, "busy" means taking a pair of heavy scissors, cutting out a golf-ball-sized chunk, and putting it in a dish, with some sea water, under, of course, a microscope.

Through the lenses, the first thing I do is assess my forceps' points. They are sharpened well. There's no need to stop this expedition into the Pacific Ocean floor just to file them down, you guessed it, under a dissecting microscope. A research experience usually begins with safety training—chemicals, broken glass, needles, razor blades, electrical wires—anything that would not only hurt someone, but perhaps just as importantly, not inspire legal action against the institution. One safety lesson in this particular laboratory goes completely against human reflexes: if we drop something, we generally try to catch it. But if you drop your forceps, let 'em fall. Why? If you try to catch a properly sharpened pair of forceps, the points will go right through your hand and, depending on what you've been picking apart, may carry with them exotic bacteria to challenge your immune system or something allergenic enough to feel like a bee sting.

But once they leave your hand, perfectly sharpened forceps tend to obey Sod's Law, which actually is the familiar Murphy's Law but applied to dropped objects, especially jellybread (which always lands jelly side down). Likewise, dropped forceps will always land on their perfectly sharpened points. The only positive outcome of this event is that you get to buy some new forceps, or, if you've obeyed Sam's Law, you get another pair out of a drawer. Who is Sam and what is his Law? Sam is Sam Bristow, my stepfather, and his law is exceedingly simple: if you find something you like (clothes that fit, forceps that sharpen nicely, etc.), buy a lifetime's supply. Sam's Law applies, also, to kelp holdfast. Once you mess with it, then you either move to the coast to become a marine invertebrate zoologist or you order it every semester, finding any excuse to do so. For one who studies animals, kelp holdfast is the

68

ultimate "something you like." The only problem is that like all natural phenomena, you can "have" it only so long as you leave it mostly undisturbed, making its own kinds of peace with whatever environmental niche it's occupied through eons of evolutionary history. Fortunately, at least for the foreseeable future, the Monterey Abalone Company plays the role of father with a jar of grass and water: a deliverer of wonder.

Among the more seemingly inspirational microscope exercises that ever popped into my brain is one involving kelp holdfast and a hundred college students who had no clue about, and thus, through no fault of their own, no appreciation for what lives among the tangled, fibrous, mat. Kelp therefore becomes a model for encounter between complete ignorance and total exotica, the former produced, if not fomented, by popular culture, the latter produced by default, a result of macroscopic algae just hanging on to the Pacific Ocean floor. For an instructor, a hundred first-year college students in an introductory required course named Organismic Biology present an interesting challenge. Outside the classroom their lives are awash in work, significant other texts and twitters, helicopter parents, sports talk, booze, clothes, fractured time, exams, volunteer gigs foisted off on them by advisers with all the answers about how to get into this professional program or that, fraternity and sorority obligations, and, of course, popular culture: *The Daily Show*, fashion, music, movies, cars ... all of it. Meanwhile, off the California coast, light years away from the hundred's past nineteen years of experience, a brown alga, genus *Macrocystis*, grows in forests, anchored to the bottom by a tangled mass of fibers, doing exactly what it's been doing for at least several hundred million years. In between the understandably clueless kid and the marine forest is a company that sells natural stuff, a FedEx truck, an airplane, and, of course, a lens. A phone call to Monterey brings the participants together. A teacher's question is: how do we match complete ignorance with total exotica? In other words, what should we do with our lenses?

The answer to this question is somewhat hidden, but it's as old as our species, and perhaps even older: look at something new, something never imagined, something that will capture, then hold, a college kid's attention. Although we really don't know for certain what it took to keep our pre-human ancestors meaningfully occupied, we can make some educated guesses: large carnivores, flowering cycles of food plants, rival clans, mating rituals, the elements—the same things that currently dictate lives and fates of other potential prey such as antelopes, rabbits, and baboons. All of these factors required serious attention to detail on the part of *Australopithecus afarensis* and *Homo erectus*, retention and application of knowledge derived from experience, and curiosity. Yes, curiosity sustains attention, at least when given the opportunity.

With today's college students, curiosity is under constant assault; everything that seems to define the life of a young, Third Millennium, American erodes curiosity, especially curiosity about the natural world. Digital music, cell phones, computers, aggressive and charismatic organized religion, talk radio, pervasive and ubiquitous sports babble, fill their lives, dull their senses, and convert these highly intelligent primates into receivers instead of seekers, animals with answers instead of questions. None of them, it often seems, would know what to do when faced with a bear at the cave door. Kelp holdfast, unlike the bear, comes without teeth, claws, and appetite, but like the bear, demands some serious attention to detail.

The lens now becomes a weapon in a teacher's war against popular culture, and an assignment is the trigger. It's the same assignment my father delivered—absent the $7000 tuition and $1300 fees required to walk into my classroom and another $7000 to live in a dorm down the street—when he filled up that jar with grass and water then put it up on a shelf in the garage for two weeks. But instead of a jar of fetid seething life, it's a tangled mat of brown algae, and instead of paramecia, it's an equally seething menagerie of microscopic creatures that, given the past experience of these students, might as well be from outer space. But these creatures are not from outer space; they're from inner space. Something vaguely familiar starts to creep up through the endless talk with some significant other in calculus class half a block away. Yes, I remember, maybe from a childhood visit to some museum, what a starfish looks like. No, I had no idea there were so many of them, that they were so tiny, that they moved with such grace, that a brittle star was not the same as an asteroid, that alive they are so much different than their pictures, that their impact on my senses when they're alive is so much different than when they're dead. Nature does its trick, if given the chance.

In possession of kelp holdfast, a dissecting microscope quickly becomes the experiential equivalent of that funeral seat next to an erstwhile vocal music major. What a grown man with a PhD cannot easily do from the front of a large auditorium, a living brittle star does instantly and unknowingly, namely, capture the full attention of a modern college student whose inundation with info-babble has rendered him or her immune to bio-babble from just another talking head. Thus on a Friday afternoon I plot my revenge against cell phones, the Internet, Bill O'Reilly and Rush Limbaugh. I meet with my laboratory instructors. Kelp holdfast arrives next Tuesday, I warn them. They smile; they know what's about to happen. I continue: this year we're making a dichotomous key, and I'm paying points for participation. The smiles turn ornery; this is going to be fun, watching what happens when it suddenly becomes important to actually describe some truly exotic creature accurately, then make a decision about how to help someone else figure out what it actually is.

A dichotomous key is a tool almost as ancient as hammers. I would never be surprised to discover, in some European museum, a tablet with a dichotomous key carved into it, now on display after being dredged up from the muck in someplace like Lake Neuchetal. And like a hammer, a dichotomous key retains its usefulness in the face of exponentially changing technology. "What is it?" is still the most pervasive and enduring question in biology. A dichotomous key is the device we use to answer that question, or more properly, to try to answer biology's most pervasive and enduring question. What is a dichotomous key? It's a series of statements, usually presented in couplets, that allow one to choose between two different observed conditions. If you are trying to identify adult mosquitoes, for example, the first thing you'll be asked to observe is wing venation:

1. Second marginal cell of wing short, less than half
   as long as its petiole. . . . . *Uranotaenia*
1A. Second marginal cell of wing as long or longer
   than its petiole 2

Obviously anyone with a mosquito under the microscope and biology's most enduring and pervasive question in hand must learn some structure (second marginal cell, petiole). But once we learn what to look for, the decision is easy. The word "petiole" is derived by analogy from botany; a petiole is that short stem between a leave and a twig. A cell is an enclosed space, in this case, enclosed by wing veins you can see easily, with a lens, and looking somewhat like a leaf. "Marginal" means at the edge, in this case ending at the edge of the wing. Right away you can decide, simply by studying a wing and learning a few simple words, whether your mosquito belongs to the genus *Uranotaenia*. If it does, then you're faced with another choice: give up whatever plans for the future you might have and spend the rest of your life studying *Uranotaenia* species because they are so unforgivingly beautiful and mysterious, or go on to the second couplet (2). Most students go to the second couplet, a commitment to a series of additional couplets.

Back in Nebraska, brittle stars and worms that a day earlier were living in the Pacific Ocean now hide from fluorescent lights in a downtown university laboratory. The worms all have spines. These spines often are barbed, like miniature harpoons; they're in tufts sticking out of lobes on the sides of each body segment and they pulse in and out, slowly stabbing, into the water. Most of these worms have eyes; all have more long lobes around their mouths, and tentacles, and shimmering skin that reflects iridescence up through the glass lenses and into the crystalline lenses of a young man's eyes, now just beginning to understand the difficulty of his assignment: make a dichotomous key to the animals that live in kelp holdfast. He's never seen any of these animals before; none of them would come to mind if asked to define the word "animal." The vast majority are tiny, and even the larger ones have microscopic structural features that must be used to distinguish them from one another. Barbs on spines you can see only through a powerful lens, shapes of tentacles, numbers and locations of eyespots, and jaws, with backward hooking teeth—all features of the natural world that this young person had no idea existed—suddenly become important.

Why are these worm parts important? The answer is a mentor's standard: they are models for life's larger tasks. They're also now linked to this kid's grade, too, but that's a minor issue. In addition to an amazing diversity of mobile marine worms, otherwise known as "errant polychaetes," there are microscopic crustaceans of various kinds, hermit crabs in tiny shells, brittle stars, sea urchins, tube worms with feathery anterior ends and tubes made of protein, or sand grains, or secreted calcium carbonate, or combinations of these components, a dozen species of snails, peanut worms, bryozoans, sponges, nematodes, an occasional flatworm so beautiful and graceful that it totally rearranges your perception of flatworms, anemones and hydrozoans, and protozoans that are superficially similar to some you'd see in a Nebraska roadside ditch a couple of weeks after a midsummer toad-strangler thunderstorm. Our pre-med who enrolled in Biology, thinking (hoping?) that he'd learn something about heart and kidney function, now sits in front of his microscope wondering whether he's been dumped onto an alien planet. In a sense he has; when viewed through a microscope, Earth, to the uninformed, unwary, and uninterested, is indeed alien. So I hand this kid an assignment that will stick: make a dichotomous key to the animals in kelp holdfast.

His first task, sitting before a microscope, looking at Earth in a way he's never done before, is to decide what's important. He's been taught how to make such decisions for the past eighteen or nineteen years by his mother, his public school teachers, and his church, and occasionally by real police, too. Depending on who he is, and where and with whom he grew to college age, his criteria for deciding what's important can vary enormously, from skin color, to religion, to sexual orientation, to politics, to age, to national origin—all those factors which, by law, we are encouraged to ignore when making decisions that involve public funds. Furthermore, by virtue of his own labor, and his own decisions, he will see the ultimate consequences of what he's done with this invertebrate menagerie because a dichotomous key is just that: two-branched. Once he makes a decision, and follows a branch, he can't leap across to the other, but instead must again choose between branches 2A and 2B, for example, having already chosen between 1A and 1B. His second choice is constrained by his first, and his third by his second, and so on. Finally, although our pre-med in paradise will, by the end of this exercise, be a relative expert among pre-meds, his product—the dichotomous key—is really intended for the ignorant, the next kid who, texting his significant other, walks in and sits down in front of a kelp holdfast with the full intention of slipping out of lab early. Good luck.

It's a little bit of a stretch, but not an extreme one, to consider dichotomous keys analogous to trajectories of individual lives. Choices are always constrained by prior ones. In 1959, for example, when my girlfriend Karen Oneth, who I considered my intended wife, told me she'd never marry a lawyer I decided right then not to go to law school; we got married two years later. That decision was the equivalent of taking branch 1B of life's dichotomous key; 1B was "ornithologist," but George M. Sutton, Research Professor of Zoology at the University of Oklahoma made the next choice for me (2B) by telling me to go get a MS first, then he'd consider taking me under his wing (sorry; had to use that metaphor!). Another faculty member at OU, Harley Brown, also made my decision (3A) by offering me a master's thesis project. Two years later when I asked John Teague Self, a parasitologist, if I could work under his guidance toward a doctorate, that was choice 4A, which led me to couplet 5, with the options: 5A = protozoa; 5B = worms. In retrospect, the experience of working with Harley Brown on nutrition and development of a ciliated protozoan, *Dileptus anser*, made this choice an easy one: I took 5A and promptly sat down at a microscope to look at protozoa—seriously, professionally—for the rest of my life.

Our pre-med with his eyes to the lens doesn't have the luxury of hindsight, but he does have an aquarium full of exotic mystery and someone to tell him that it's okay to wallow in that mess of stuff for three hours. A simple phrase— "Today we're going to make a dichotomous key."—coupled with the fact that these words are uttered in a laboratory where any and all activities are assumed to be graded, establishes credibility. It's now okay to visit your alien planet, the one you grew up on, at least to college age, and furthermore, because the job is so large you now have nineteen assistants, who are really only the other students in lab. In the next three hours, all twenty will be looking through lenses, making decisions about what they see through lenses, drawing pictures intended to convey information, talking to others about sights and decisions, and by the end of that period, they'll have formed a habit: picking up a lens for a closer look at something, yes, out of habit. The habit sticks because it's one of the oldest, most well-known, artists' tricks, one known and practiced regularly by every photographer who ever picked up a camera and studied it carefully, thinking to himself or herself: I wonder what this thing can actually do? The answer is: look at stuff in different ways.

If you look at the same object from different angles, in different conditions of light, at different magnifications, in the company of various other items, over an extended period of time, then that object becomes transformed into something that is almost, or at least can seem to be, alive. It develops a personality ("This chair goes best in that corner."); it acquires a history ("Remember when I had it reupholstered?" "Yes, but I liked it better before."); it heightens your awareness of certain events and socio-economic conditions ("I can't believe we only paid $100 for it. Now that place is out of business."); and it becomes an active participant in your own life ("Found a couple of quarters when I vacuumed under the cushion; reminds me of visiting my grandfather's house and finding coins in the sofa where he'd taken a nap.") When lenses, metaphorical or otherwise, are involved, encrusted shells behave just like living room chairs in the sense that they connect you with past experiences and train your eye—your mental or physical eye—for future encounters with the unknown. In higher education, we call that training "acquisition of transferable skills."

What metaphorical lenses don't necessarily train you for is encounter with those creatures living at the lower limits of resolution, a group that includes most of the occupants of fruit jars filled with water and grass then left to stew for a couple of weeks. These so-called "infusion cultures," assembled by anyone anywhere on Earth, useful for purposes ranging from mystification of preteens to the writing of doctoral dissertations, and costing virtually nothing (fruit jar, grass, water), make kelp holdfast look almost manageable. Only the amebas move slowly enough to track easily with lenses that magnify a thousand times. Everything else careens at speeds best measured in body lengths per second, with no discernable purpose or destination. Where did they really come from? You ask. Were they there, in the grass, before I put that stuff in the jar? Were they there, in the water from my faucet, the very water that I drink every day, before I made this mess? Did they ride in on the air, the same air I breathe continuously? Did I inadvertently make a community with a defined life and compressed history? This last question is easy to answer: yes. In another week, there may be occupants not present now, and some of the dominant forms will have disappeared from the mix. In a month, nothing you recognize today will still be around. If microorganisms could think and write, you'd see the rise and fall of a great jar nation in only six weeks, and the lesson of limited resources would stick in your mind until you became President of another great nation, the one your grandfather came to when things became intolerable in Bohemia, or Ireland, or Sudan, or ... Mexico.

If microorganisms could write, their story might also seem vaguely familiar to a work laden with metaphorical baggage. With your lenses, you have fallen, Alice-like, into a round hole, and just as Alice-like, the results completely alter your perception of reality. At first, the denizens of this tiny world reveal no sense of purpose, no sense of direction, no awareness of past, present, or future, nothing that connects them to any familiar sign posts or behavioral traits by which we negotiate the realms of money, health, military adventure, agriculture, politics, sex, sports, or religion. You do not belong in this realm you have just entered; you have no idea what processes actually govern its existence, what its inhabitants do for a living, or how they got there. Only your education prevents you from deciding, like long-ago ancestors would have done, that they simply appeared spontaneously. Slowly, very slowly, your evolved internal wiring, established neural circuits, and past experiences, begin to reassert themselves. You are, after all, a human being; if you have any power at all, it is to impose your will on nature, at least in terms of interpretation. They eat; they mate; and, they fight, just like I do, you think. Suddenly they sort themselves out into a pattern you recognize: thousands of them, all vibrating and smacking into one another, have gathered around an air bubble. Oh, you think; they need air; they want air. You have absolutely no idea whatsoever what they need; they are incapable of want. Your conclusion is fantasy. Five minutes have now passed. What you have seen through this lens is an irresistible drive to impose your own guiding mythology on the natural world and thus believe that you have, in fact, also imposed your will.

But you cannot control what happens in this jar of grass, water, and time without creating a human work of art. You can kill everything with heat or hydrochloric acid; you can change the community makeup by adding a handful of rice or fish food; you can decide whether to let the water evaporate or keep it filled to a certain mark; and, if you're really a masochist, you can try to isolate one of the community members in "pure" culture. But once you perform any of these acts, you've created something that would not have otherwise occurred naturally. The blasé ease with which you add that handful of rice mimics our approach to nature in general, whether it be mowing the yard, planting trees, digging a ship channel through the Mississippi River Delta, or burning Amazon forest at the rate of fifty acres a minute, year after year. Eventually the infusion culture will collapse, no matter what you do. Eventually there will be no more movement under the lens.

The difference between your jar and the tropical forest is one of the big take-home lessons: you can start another jar, generating that mystery at will, but you can never replace the biological diversity lost when that forest is gone.

Introduction to "The Horse"

In 1989, Ted Turner created the Turner Tomorrow Fellow-ship Award for a "fiction work offering creative and positive solutions to global problems." The winner was to be offered a $500,000 advance and publishing contract. I immediately began work on my entry, entitled *The Ginkgo*, with the full intent of winning that competition. To make a long story short, I didn't win, or even finish my book, before Daniel Quinn claimed the prize with *Ishmael*, a novel he'd been working on for at least ten years. But I eventually finished, then rewrote several times, *The Ginkgo*, a story about a college student from a ranch in western Nebraska who comes to the university and ends up writing four essays about a single ginkgo tree.

This student had to be a female, in fact a very intelligent and rather secular one, for a whole variety of purely narrative reasons. In my mind, this book is a visionary coming-of-age story about the burden of traditions, the powerful lifetime influence of a liberal education, and the human condition. I envisioned it being the next *Zen and the Art of Motorcycle Maintenance*, at least commercially and in terms of becoming a cult piece. My literary agent, however, called it "an evocative book about ideas, exactly the kind of thing the American book-buying public is becoming increasingly impatient with" and promptly declined to handle it. Similar opinions were evi-dently held by the next forty-two publishers who rejected it. All that backstory aside, *The Ginkgo*, subtitled *An Intellectual and Visionary Coming-of-Age*, remains my best work, ever, and in my highly biased opinion, the most important; it's also now available on Amazon.com and Kindle.com.

In *The Ginkgo*, this coed comes to the university, is asked to write four papers about a single plant, a typical activity for my large freshman classes, indeed an exercise that we have done for years, although the specific assignments differ from year to year. As a result of her performance, she is selected by her prof as penance for all his past sins, namely, all those cases in which he's allowed, or even helped, a truly brilliant young person become a physician or other health care professional with a real job, instead of becoming a poet or philosopher who could, and would, be the intellectual leader our nation so severely needs. You can see immediately where the "creative and positive solutions to global problems" part comes in; if there is anything this nation needs in the Third Millennium, it is ideas, especially good ones.

To quote from the prologue to *The Ginkgo*, which I rewrote after my agent declined it: "What happens to nations that get increasingly impatient with evocative books about ideas? Why can't I get that phrase out of my mind? I walk downtown. The sidewalks are filled with normal, everyday, people—lawyers, housewives, businessmen and businesswomen, panhandlers, college kids, and nondescripts. Are they *all* impatient with evocative books about ideas? What are they not impatient with? Murder, narcotics, war? Or are they not impatient with money, politics, agriculture, health, the military, sex, sports, or religion, the very subjects she was not allowed to write about throughout the year she went exploring a tree, a museum, a sculpture garden, an art gallery? Is it indeed possible that this society has degenerated into one so impatient with ideas that it will neither read nor buy an evocative book about them? I don't believe this is the case. I believe my fellow citizens are vitally interested in ideas. Why else would they flock, in droves, to churches? Why else would they gravitate to certain politicians? Why else would they be so quick to categorize then dehumanize their fellow humans? Believe me, we are very interested in ideas; they are the hands that guide our acts, all of them, both good and evil."

In many ways, *The Ginkgo* is symbolic of my teaching experience at UNL, and especially the emotional impact of spending all those years at the Cedar Point Biological Station in Keith County. Karen and I watched our children grow up out there; we came to be in awe of the subtle beauty, especially the early morning and late afternoon landscape colors, the sounds and smells, and the generous landowners whose property my students used regularly; and, we eventually developed an idyllic view of the Sandhills. This view developed, of course, because we were intellectual visitors, not residents who had to make a living from the arid high plains. The romance of western Nebraska is thus a luxury; all of our friends out there work extremely hard, and most of the time this work is outright physical labor, always with the chance of injury or devastating weather, and rarely with any escape except for that hour in church on Sunday mornings.

Much of *The Ginkgo* takes place in the Sandhills, on a couple of ranches, but the book really is about teaching, mentoring in its most challenging, yet rewarding, way. Naturally, because the Cedar Point instructional program has offered a lifetime's challenge and reward, the western Nebraska landscape and culture had to be essential elements of this story. Just as naturally, by hanging around writers and artists, often because of Karen's job, it never seemed unusual for a scientist to try his hand at fiction. Artists express themselves, in the process making their statements about the world whether they intend to do so or not, using whatever media seems appropriate. When a scientist believes he has something to say, something important, about the business of education, then he or she should also feel free to use any media to make such a statement. With a little luck, the product is an evocative book about ideas.

In the excerpt that follows, the prof has gone to western Nebraska in search of ideas, but in this case, the ideas are ones specifically designed to frame the assignments this student will be asked to pursue. Thus a teacher goes exploring into a student's cultural background in order to come up with the perfect teaching devices. We profs do, or at least should do, this kind of exploration every day. What we don't do regularly is drive a thousand miles for the sole purpose of spending time in the landscape and society where our students grow up simply so we can come up with the right test questions; such thousand-mile trips happen only in fiction.

Other characters mentioned in "The Horse" are members of the Johannes and Spindler clans. Carl Johannes owns a massive amount of land; he and his wife have produced a number of beautiful and intelligent daughters, but no sons. Dalton Spindler owns a much smaller ranch, but he and his wife have four sons, ranging from the hard-working and responsible Terry to the ne'er-do-well Gerry. Carl Johannes has his eyes not only on Spindler property, but also on the ranch where *The Ginkgo* coed grew up before she came to the university. You can see immediately where this story is heading. The Johannes girls are all barrel racers with magnificent horses from their father's ranch; at least two of them have already captured their Spindler boys.

It will help in understanding one sentence in "The Horse" if you know that in the previous chapter the student—the main character in this book—has intercepted the prof on his way into a large lecture section of General Biology and demanded that he lecture about reproduction instead of the scheduled topic because another student in her dorm has tried to commit suicide by cutting her wrists as a result of an unwanted pregnancy. *The Ginkgo* deals, obviously, at least in part, with some of our nation's truly divisive hot-button issues. Now join me in a Sandhills pasture for a conversation with a horse.

The Horse

*Ai-sah idly entered the gray colt in the race
elimination contests. To his great delight it won every
heat easily. All the Kiowas were pleased ...*

—Wilbur Surtevant Nye, *Bad Medicine
& Good: Tales of the Kiowas*

Bodmer lies in a vee made by two rivers that come out of
the mountains and join in the middle of the plains. The
water then meanders eastward across another three hundred
miles of prairie, until it empties into the Missouri. An interstate highway follows the southern branch of this great river
system; the other branch cuts through the edge of a dune
ocean that begins at the Bodmer city dump and ends somewhere in the Dakotas. I suppose if you lived back in pioneer
days these topographic features would represent obstacles to
your westward migration, a series of relentless hardships that
stood between you and California. Today, California is a surrealistic parody of Dreamland, and the open country north of
Bodmer is a real life version of the American Icon—open
space, clear sky, an unmarked, unblemished, frontier. Americans are conquerors and builders; they need elbow room and
raw materials. Americans are also wives and mothers; they
need faithful hardworking husbands and well behaved children. Thus we build this house made of the nouns and adjec-
tives that we think describe Americans. Then we turn our
house into a mansion by putting people like Carl Johannes in
charge of it. Then we elect presidents who get to live in the
mythical mansion. Back home, Carl spends most of his time
working like a pack mule and managing his money with the
skill of a mob lawyer. But the rest of the country still thinks it
lives in the mansion.

At my feet are pebbles, stones pumped from the river bed,
sorted into several grades of sand and gravel, and sold to the

. . . THE TINY KANGAROO RATS I HEAR
BENEATH MY FEET AT NIGHT . . .

county for road maintenance. Graders came through, north of Bodmer, after the late August storms, erasing washouts, mile after mile, past Antelope Springs Ranch, Wounded Deer Ranch, Sandy Creek Ranch, Broken Wheel Ranch, all owned by Johannes Land and Cattle Company, that is, by Carl Johannes, patriarch and horse breeder for the Johannes girls, barrel racers. Johannes land starts three miles west of where I'm parked. The property line is marked by a concrete box culvert covered with a cattle guard. Old tire halves are nailed to gate posts either side of the guard in an attempt to keep braver steers from slipping around the pipe covered pit and wandering onto a neighbor's land. Fence posts are of Osage Orange—Beau d'Arc—brought up from Kansas. These posts last a hundred years; you can't drive a staple into them so the barbed wire is wired to the gnarly, crooked, spindly looking stakes. A "no hunting" sign hangs to the right of the Johannes gate. On the other side of the fence, a similar sign warns the traveler he's passing from Johannes property and onto the ranch where the young woman who selected a ginkgo tree as her avenue into the future spent her childhood.

In the distance, sun reflects off the valley floor, off rivulets running around sand and gravel bars and through trees that have encroached on the channel. The river was once a mile wide here, but what used to be a flood plain is now hay meadow. Upstream dams have cut the flow; some describe these dams as "progress;" others call them "make work for BuRec." Whatever they are, they've allowed humanity to control the floodplain. A lush blanket of deep green extends from the cottonwoods up to a long natural terrace that marks the valley's edge. From where I'm parked, I can see five or six miles both east and west; all along the river, ranchers have used the plain for hay meadow. Around my ankles, digger bees dart erratically in low, tight, figure eights over the sandy roadbed; bees might have been making their little chimney burrow entrances on this hillside for centuries before someone came along and put a road through the Ginkgo property. Then the bees simply dug where they'd always dug, but now they're in the road. In mid-afternoon on the road north of Bodmer, digger bees are the only active creatures I see; they make the only noise I can hear.

Below me, down the terrace, sits a stucco house with a long front porch, low sloping dark roof that completely overhangs the porch, and large, rectangular, front windows. The steps emerge from between two half-columns topped with flat, square, concrete slabs. The window frames are wide, and wooden. Frank Lloyd Wright created this basic design, called, appropriately, Prairie Style. I'm sure this particular house is not a Wright; the state's three Wright buildings are well known, and preserved. This one is an excellent mimic, however. And, it's well preserved, but not by the state. My student evidently comes from a careful, intelligent, and responsible family. Good, I think. Those are excellent qualities; they will serve her well in the weeks to come. One must remain careful, responsible, and very alert, in a museum, a sculpture garden, an art gallery.

I wonder if the Ginkgos know the architectural history of their home. What difference would it make in their lives, if they did? I don't know. Architecture is one of the most subtle—although the architects would argue this point—and sometimes subversive, of arts. Every day she awoke to the shadows and angles produced by this house. In the summer, prairie sounds drifted in through the open window—meadowlarks, redwing blackbirds, their *scru-u-ree-e-ely* calls carrying up from the center of their territories, down in the marsh. In December, sleet banged against the glass, as she looked out toward the barns and thought about horses, and machinery, and wondered what would become of it all when her parents died. And in April, she'd watch dark green clouds developing in the west. When the clouds turned green, they'd go into the cellar.

Down the terrace from the house, and to the west, is a garage. This one is corrugated steel, relatively new, with a pair of large sliding doors that hang from rails. People out here don't put cars in the garage; they put their work machines in there, close to the stand-up bench, anvil, metal lathe, and vise. Acetylene tanks are on a dolly; they can be wheeled out in the yard, if necessary, to weld a broken trailer hitch. Cans of kerosene, carburetor cleaner, brake fluid, fill the shelves, along with cases of oil, hydraulic hoses, v-belts. Outside the garage, two 500-gallon tanks—one gasoline, the other diesel—rest on a head-high angle-iron frame. Further to the west stands the main barn.

Beyond the barn are horse corrals. A double horse trailer is parked nearby, empty, waiting, perhaps, like its intended passengers, for some excitement. Thrills are few and far between around Bodmer: branding's bawling mayhem, a thunderhead's explosive electric violence, a coal train derailment's earth-shaking screaming steel rumble, all exclamation points in the essay of life along the western rivers. The rest of the story is a linear, controlled, narrative: hard work in phases bound to planetary cycles, sermons predictably focused on obedience, and a matrix of debt and credit in which all things agricultural are embedded. Only the horses seem free. I look to the north; two roans, a paint, and a dappled gray have gathered at the windmill and its overflow pool. They stomp their feet, gently, flick their tails, and stare at me, snorting.

I try to guess which one is hers, which one used to feel her saddle thrown upon his back, her hands pulling the cinch tight around his belly, and is now longing for that familiar physical contact while she's off in the city struggling with strange ideas. They're like barrels, old friend, always waiting for you to try your skills at negotiating the paths around them. He pounds out of the gate, mud flying, wind whipping his mane. He feels her legs, strong, squeezing him, her boot heels digging into his ribs, her crotch slamming against his back, her quirt stinging on his flank, and her soul and spirit coursing through his blood. His slather flies; the steel bar touches his lip; in all the hurtling violence, the gentle hint of pressure seems no different from her soft strokes on his forehead; he feels her lean; the orange oil drum rings with the pop of a flying clod. Go! Go! Run, horse; Run! Go! Go! Go, horse; Go! Beat that goddamn Johannes girl! Beat her ass! Win, baby! Win, goddamnit! WIN!

How can it be so fun, where you've gone? How can you leave me? Am I not good enough to fit between your legs and thrust with all my might at those corners you must turn to win? We can beat her; we can beat the odds and beat the time

5 THE HORSE

and beat the goddamn Johannes girl, if that's what you want! Three barrels! In all these fields, in all this rain and sun and wind and snow, the gray-green prairie grass, the tiny kangaroo rats I hear beneath my feet at night, the creaking of our windmill, the frogs in our stock tank, in all this free and wonderful life we have, those three barrels are something you've contrived, something out of your world that we can do together! But I can also take you to the Indian graves, to the places where I know they killed the bison, for I can still smell their bones, buried in the sand! I can take you out of sight of fences, where you can sit, and think, and let your mind go back to long ago. On the far hill I see another; he's as much of a stranger to me as his rider is to you; you don't wear a feather; your painted hand print doesn't mark my chest. Yet across the valley we can talk with our eyes—that ghost man with a feathered spear, and you, my rider. I can smell that other horse; his scent lingers from the last century. Don't you feel their presence? See, these, too, are things that we can do together.

I remember when you were small and your father first put you on my back. Then you grew up and we went chasing barrels that never moved. What were we after? I only understand tangible, solid, real things, like rocks and plants and animals. We never caught anything in the barrel races. I hate that steel trailer, but I go there only because you want me to, and I know there will be play at the end of our trip. And now you've gone to chase ideas. Ideas, my Mistress? What are ideas? Are they anything like the barrels? Do we need to beat the goddamn Johannes girl at ideas, too? Come home. I miss you. I stand by the well tank, watching the flies, the beetles dig in cow shit as the sun goes down, and I miss your weight, your voice, your hands. I hear the coyotes late at night, and smell the thunderheads, and then I miss your footsteps, your presence in the air. Come home. Or send for me. I can help you. Are there three ideas, as many as barrels? Come home.

"She can't come home, friend."

My voice is damped by the openness, the total lack of walls from which to echo. The words ring in my ears. I look in all directions, east and west, north and south, into the sky and down at the ground. I am the only human I see. Houses and barns are evidence that someone has been here in the past, but they could be abandoned, fossils, for all the activity around them. Only the digger bees are moving and making noise. Then from somewhere, far off in the distance, a killdeer calls. The piercing low whistle sounds wavy, as if filtered through the heat waves rising off the roadbed. The horse stomps and snorts; the others with him do the same.

"She can never come back. She may stand with you in the pasture, and ride with you to the far horizon, but it will never be the same again."

It's stupid for a grown man, a university professor, a scientist, to feel as if he's communicating with a horse. But suddenly I know which one is hers. I walk through the wiry grass, the hard grassland legumes, until I'm standing by the fence. His eyes watch my progress. The others back away, but he waits. I have never failed to be awed by the power of large animals. Does he smell the fact that she's been to my office? I admit the possibility; one never makes unsupported assumptions about creatures who live in worlds apart from ours. I run my hand down his forehead, my fingers through his forelock, letting the coarse hair fall over the back of my hand. He pushes at me, searching for my palm.

"All I have are greetings, friend. And she doesn't even know I'm here to pass them along."

The others come back to the fence. They can tell I'm from the city; I'm not behaving correctly. Out here, men are supposed to have a bridle in their hands, if they walk up to a horse. And what follows, is a secret rite of The West: Cowboy Saddles His Horse And Rides Off To Do Some Hard Work With Cattle. When I get back home, I must ask her whether she ever got to rope the calves and pull them out of the herd at branding time, whether she's ridden this one into that dirty violence, whether she's been allowed to occupy the second highest position in her culture: Roper at the Branding.

Already I know the answer: no. She would never be allowed to drive her pickup along the sandy roads, down through the valley over to the Johannes place, hauling the dappled gray in a rusty red trailer with the requisite amount of litter and manure and a few dents in it, bouncing over the cattle guards

5 THE HORSE

along with the other three dozen neighbors, all heading for the Johannes branding. She would never get to stick that wad of snuff in her lower lip, get up on the gray, her tight sweaty leather gloves gripping the stiff rope, then ride out into the big corral, milling around with the neighbor men, swinging their loops, waiting, waiting for the herd being driven through the west pasture by neighbors.

A thousand head being pushed toward the corral resemble nothing so much as an enemy battalion being led into ambush. The dark seething mass rolls over the pasture like a rumbling, complaining lava flow, a giant strung-out dirty hairy amoeba stomping up the meadowlarks and grasshoppers, raising a cloud of sandy dust, splattering wet green manure, but bawling, a thousand head bawling, the cows lowing, deep, the calves higher, wavering, each with its own voice, a small sea of mothers and children rounded up and shoved, inexorably, inevitably, toward that massive trap of weathered boards, toward that hot iron, the needle, the speculum, and finally, for the little bulls, the knife. Periodically some cowboy dashes out to run a cow back into the herd. There are no big bulls in this group, only females and their offspring. Ahead, the corral gates are pulled open, wide, gaping. Ropers watch, waiting, silently, for the burning and cutting to start.

The herd slams through the gate and into the corral. The noise is thundering, the motion incessant and seething. Then the separation begins. Wide-eyed, slobbering, stumbling, with swollen udders and still swollen bellies, the cows are slapped, and blocked from their calves by dashing chasing horses and men, scrambling to get out of the way of a hurtling cow, her eyes bulging, hitting the gray boards, sending shock waves all along the fence to the loading chute, then pounding out into the pasture to join the others milling, and calling for their calves, and rubbing against one another, in a big amorphous mass of beef and flies in the hot morning sun.

Then the burning and cutting begins. A dozen cowboys swing their ropes. The horses are perfect machines, stepping into the chaos, placing their feet so carefully and quickly until the loop flies toward the ground. Instantly the horse and rider back up, then turn. The rope is tight around the calf's heel.

The young bull is dragged out of the herd, out into the dirt and manure. Roper at the Branding. She would never get to be Roper at the Branding. No. The ginkgo writer would be a holder, the lowest job on the cultural hierarchy, one fit for young boys, or ranch girls who don't want to cook, and for city slickers out in the High Country for a tiny taste of the Legend.

Her father rides the dappled gray.

She waits for the next calf. Her little brother, a ninth-grader at Bodmer High, waits beside her. The big horse stomps by, the rope stretched, singing, dirt flying. The calf is dragged on its side, sliding past her. She grabs the hind hoof, feels the rope slacken—the gray has responded to her move. She glances up, into her horse's eyes, and flings the loop back onto the ground at his feet. Already her father gathers in the coils, the gray backing up, stepping quickly, lightly, his eyes focused on the action. She shoves her boot into the calf's crotch, pulls on the leg, but it's too late. Her brother loses his grip at the front. His knee slips off the neck; a cactus pad is jammed into the back of his hand; and the calf is loose, twisting, fighting, turning back on her, while all round, through the noise, the laughter burns. A hoof slams into her leg. How can they be so strong? she wonders; are they wild animals? She doesn't think her little brother is that strong, that he could kick her so hard, yet he seems as big as this calf. Her brother tries to throw it down but the animal shakes him off. Another hoof digs into her stomach. Dirty fur smashes into her mouth; she spits manure and sand. Then it's over. Except for the laughter. And she's sad, because they're laughing at the boy, not her. She's not supposed to wrestle calves; he is. And a dozen years from now, if she's still here in the hills north of Bodmer, she'll be cooking, back at the ranch house, and waiting for the cutting and burning to end, while the kid who couldn't hold a calf's front leg, or keep his knee on its neck, will be Roper at the Branding.

Her gray has caught the one who got away; her father chases the dodging, skittering, little bull back into the corral. Then quick as a rattlesnake strike, the loop flies into the stomping, running, milling mass of legs, and just as surely as the snake's strike, the calf is once again flipped on its side, and dragged back out of the herd, its eyes rolling, its mouth covered with white foam spit. She grabs her brother by the shoulders.

"Here! You take the heel! And if you let him go again I'm going to bust your ass into a million pieces!"

She shoves him into the dirt under the rope and pounces on the head, plants her knee along the jaw, and wrenches the foreleg back against the heaving ribs. She feels the heat, behind her back. She puts her hand over the calf's muzzle, holding its face in the dirt. From the corner of her eye, she sees the leather glove, the iron rod, and the red hot cylinder. Then, next to her hand, the cylinder is shoved down over a little stub of horn and pushed, burning, and twisted, burning, until the sour and stinging hair smoke swirls up around her face, and the flames lash against her jeans, and still the red hot iron is twisted into the calf's head until she sees the barren skull bone, burned. At her right knee, another iron is pushed into the side, and another puff of flames and hair smoke engulfs her, choking, stinking. And when it clears, she sees her little brother, his dirty boot jammed into between the calf's legs, and the knife, in the bowlegged old rancher's hand, the patriarch Johannes' hand, helping his neighbor and expecting the same in return. The blade slices into the scrotum. Carl Johannes digs his fingers around into the cut until he finds the testicles, and the swollen ducts attached, then pulls them out, and cuts them off, and throws them into a metal pot. Another neighbor jams a needle into the calf's flank. A kid marks the hair with a big block of chalk. A man grabs the ear, slips it into a cutter, and clips a vee shaped slice from the edge, then rivets a red tag through the other ear. Calf 164. Run to your mother, Number 164. Welcome to the American West. The kid slaps the calf as it wobbles, then trots, out into the pasture to find the cow.

One of the Johannes girls sits on the wooden railing, watching. Under a calico, tightly tapered blouse her chest is pulsing with the excitement. But back in the city, the pregnant one hesitates, blinks a stinging tear, then, with all her strength, jams the razor blade across the blue vein beneath her ivory skin.

I breathe in deeply. The air out here is clean. The smells are sage and sunflowers. I toy with the idea of driving up to the house, introducing myself, then explaining my presence in terms of insects, all as an excuse for meeting her mother, and father, and little brother. Maybe I should talk about grasshoppers instead of dragonflies. If you say you're studying grasshoppers, then people in this part of the country think you're on an important mission. To them, "study" means "find a way to kill."

Our default conclusions about others' pursuits might also merit serious study. To me, "study" means "transport your mind away to dreamland. Take yourself to another planet— the one occupied by insects, or, for that matter, ginkgo trees." No. I won't go meet her father. I won't ask if he's been Cutter at the Johannes Branding, nor why being Roper at his own branding is so important to him. For today, I'm satisfied to have met her horse.

Dragonflies dart, then hover over the well tank, poised, ready strike at anything small enough to be smashed and ripped by those deadly jaws. Out of habit, I acknowledge the familiar species—my friends, the wild things that lend scholarly substance to my career. Damselflies, the dragonflies' delicate cousins, dance over nearby weeds and grass next to the overflow. A black beetle crawls through the sand toward a flop of dried cow manure. A parasitic wasp, its long ovipositors coiling and uncoiling, searches along a weathered board. The world is a rich and busy place for my kind of people. I walk back to my car. The drive home will take seven hours, enough time to slowly absorb the enormous power of a single picture behind a bar, to properly assess the immovable traditions from which we spring, and to assemble a plan for using what I've learned. Words arranged into questions and tasks, tasks designed to open two doors, one into her future, a future she must build, and the other into her past, into her traditions, traditions that she can never escape completely, but must understand, completely, before she can build her future. And all I have to work with, to build a visionary out of raw ability, are words arranged into questions and tasks. No, that's wrong; I also have a museum and an art gallery.

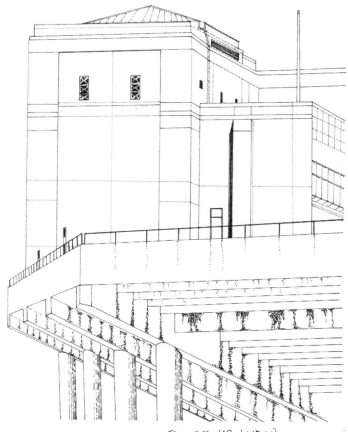

MEMORIAL STADIUM FROM THE LAB WINDOW

The Firm

A good reputation is more valuable than money.
—Publilius Syrus, *Maxim*
(first century B.C.)

An instructor says, 'My worry is that you'll become educated beyond your obedience.'
—John Rolfe Gardiner, in his review of
Kevin Roose's *The Unlikely Disciple*

For Educational Purposes, every Employé should be taken into the Firm.
—George Ade (from *The Fable of the Subordinate Who Saw a Great Light*)

Back in the late 1970s, a year went by during which I repeatedly photocopied 230 pages of manuscript, took them down to the post office, and mailed them off to some publisher. I trusted, completely, in the wisdom of *Writer's Market*, a book that I'd bought, believing with total naïveté what various companies said about their commercial interests and feeling equally confident that the next one would snap up this piece of nonfiction literature I'd entitled *The Fundulus Chronicles*. After twenty-two rejections, a young man named Dennis Holler from St. Martin's Press called and asked if the book had been sold. I said no, it was still available, and he replied that they were interested in publishing it. I was alert enough to not say something about the previous rejections, one of which had been with a letter asking "why do you waste your postage sending us things that don't turn us on?" and tried to act calm, as he said that someone would call me back the next day. When Tom Dunne, the St. Martin's editor who accepted the book, called later, he made the verbal offer, $5000 in advance royalties, but also indicated that St. Martin's

Press didn't want to get into a bidding war. I told him to send me the contract and I'd sign it. That book eventually became *Keith County Journal*. A few weeks after it was published, I got a late afternoon phone call from someone at *Time* magazine.

"We're reviewing *Keith County Journal*," the caller said; "could you provide a photograph?"

"Sure," I replied; "what's the address? I can mail it."

"No need to mail it," she said; "just put it in an envelope somewhere that we can pick it up."

I put the picture in an envelope, wrote TIME MAGAZINE in big capital letters on the front, and put it on the floor outside my office door, leaning up against the wall. When I came to work the following morning the envelope was gone. The next time I saw that photograph it was in *Time*. A few days later I was walking back from Bennett Martin Library, in downtown Lincoln, into the teeth of a bitter February north wind, when a colleague from another department yelled at me from across the street.

"*Hey, John!! What's _____ saying about you now?!? Huh? What's _____ saying about you now?!?*"

The individual referred to as _____ was my department chair. I tend to think about this particular set of events fairly often, mainly because they seem to characterize my business, namely, that of American higher education. In this business, reputation is currency, and it can be earned, spent, created, or destroyed, just like other kinds of currency, but the worst thing you can do with it is leave it in that metaphorical bank where it earns no interest, for example in the files of your department chairman's office. In this business, reputation needs to be put to work—invested—sometimes to bring you pleasure, like a deep intellectual conversation during a quiet meal with good friends, or to recruit a student with exactly the right kind of personality into your research lab. At other times it needs to serve as a weapon, like when you use it on purpose to make another university employee uncomfortable if not downright psychologically stressed out of his or her mind. Usually, but not always, your immediate supervisor is the target. And when you need such a weapon, your picture in *Time* is the rough equivalent of a nuclear warhead.

America's universities are places where words sustain a multi-billion industry and supply a nation with expertise necessary to deliver engineering, health care, legal advice, and business acumen, all in addition to gentle help for a five-year-old trying to learn "See Spot run"—your local elementary school teachers struggling with a rapidly changing ethnic and linguistic mix. The words are those of students and professors, and they express ideas. Sometimes those words are written down on paper, or nowadays into an electronic file, and sometimes they are spoken in front of audiences ranging from a select handful to non-select hundreds. But few such words are ever spoken at a university without someone's reputation being involved. Every sentence delivered to a freshman biology class of 250 students, forty-five hours of talk over a three-month period, makes someone tell someone else either *Don't take this class!* or *Get this guy for 101 if you can!* At least one of those sentences will be repeated, verbatim, on your student evaluations at semester's end. The right twenty words uttered in an otherwise deadly boring faculty meeting can reek of scholarly insight and, often to the consternation of colleagues, direct decisions that ultimately affect thousands. On that February day in downtown Lincoln it didn't come as much of a surprise that this particular colleague would yell at me from across the street: *"Hey, John!! What's _____ saying about you now?!? Huh? What's _____ saying about you now?!?"* I knew what _____ had been saying about me. The biting north wind suddenly turned into a warm southern breeze.

Academics are generally hired to teach but expected to do research. If their research gets published in certain *journals— Nature, Science,* and the *Proceedings of the National Academy of Sciences (PNAS)* come immediately to mind—then one's scholarly reputation is greatly enhanced, especially among those for whom a paper in one of those journals is the only currency thought to buy respect. Certain kinds of scholarly reputations also are of great financial value to universities, and consequently considered, by administrators, to be particularly valuable. A ten-million-dollar grant can deliver thousands of dollars in "overhead," which is then used to remodel laboratories, provide "start-up" funds for new faculty members, and, most importantly, support the efforts to get more grants. Nowadays, large universities that don't pursue grant money as aggressively as they pursue alumni support and athletic victory should probably be considered institutionally naïve beyond description. Nowadays, large universities that don't ballyhoo their latest patents during an allotted halftime minute of some nationally-televised athletic contest probably need to hire some new public relations folks. Down in local bars where graduate students gather to watch the game, they call this ad "our Rumpelstiltskin Moment": we've spun straw into gold and everyone gets a nugget; someday. Now send your kid to our place, tuition check and credit card in hand.

Few outside The Firm, however, understand just what large externally-funded research programs cost society in terms of human resources. Fewer still understand what such programs actually accomplish for society: the production of well-educated, rational, and evidence-driven scholars. And even fewer understand that we cannot forge, or maintain, the link between research and our scientific and technological resources only with massive amounts of money and reputation. This link is a human one, made out of interpersonal relations. For example, the first thing you learn when you become a faculty member is that those thousands of young faces who walk in your front door every year are raw material from which a great nation is built. The next thing you learn is that you simply cannot predict students' futures, or their eventual contributions to society, from their appearance or their grades in BIOS 101 General Biology. And if you're smart, you'll figure out in a hurry that some of them will wander into your lab, ask what's going on, then, if there's anything interesting "going on," stick around, join in the fun, and make you famous.

But the first thing you learn when you accept a university administrative position is that all communication now comes from above, instead of from those students below, and most of it concerns money and obedience. The take-home message from all these lessons combined is that two main facets of American higher education—teaching and research—often are in conflict, potentially damaging to the young thousands eager for some undefined meaning to their lives, to the old few who live in a world built largely of money and regulations, and ultimately to the institution itself. But the conflict is not a direct one; instead, it involves competition for faculty time and ideas, with a heavy dose of dollar-worship. Nevertheless, as in any marriage of extreme convenience, these two facets of university life—teaching and research—also are mutually supportive, indeed symbiotic, often in ways never suspected, even by people who live in the ivory tower.

Regardless of whatever conflict may seem to exist between teaching and research, faculty members at colleges and universities, including those at small schools and places that fall somewhere near the bottom of *Newsweek*'s annual ranking of American institutions, need to stay in intellectual shape just as some doormat football team daily trudges off to practice and the weight room. For The Firm, research is the easiest, cheapest, and most efficient mechanism for keeping its most valuable and expensive resources—the faculty—mentally healthy, engaged in their disciplines and eager to engage students in a similar way. For example, a new species description is a non-trivial act, even though that description may be of some truly obscure protozoan discovered inside an insect that causes no agricultural damage, published in a peer-reviewed journal generally spoken of in rather disparaging terms by some department chair. In performing such an act, you learn the most important lesson gleaned from a lifetime working for The Firm: *even the most elementary piece of research often becomes an allegorical journey during which you develop a deep appreciation for the fundamental nature of inquiry.*

This last lesson—not the money, not the reputation, not the Rumpelstiltskin Moment— is why research is The Firm's life's blood. The Firm also exists to deliver such a lesson, although this *raison d'être* often is one of the first forgotten and thus the last considered when management decisions must be made, decisions such as whom to hire, who teaches what to whom, and where this teaching will take place. In most academic disciplines, publication records and success at getting grants are used as evidence of intellectual strength and performance, regardless of what kinds of personalities, often truly bizarre ones, are involved. Universities are sometimes perceived as havens for the socially incompetent, and not without reason. Behaviors necessary for a lifetime's research on anything, be it the Battles of Lexington and Concord or mating habits of tarantulas, bear no relationship whatsoever to behaviors necessary for success as a real estate agent, trial lawyer, boutique manager, newspaper reporter, advertising executive, or elementary school teacher. From watching my fellow faculty members over four decades, and observing my counterparts from other institutions, I'm convinced that research behaviors, or at least the personalities that spawn them, have a major genetic component. People end up as university professors by filtration, not by training. In the filtration process, we never ask whether those same people are so psychologically insecure and afraid of anything but their own pet projects that they can't look up and say "hello" to a student in the hallway.

But American higher education grew to its present stature, at least to a significant degree, by claiming the importance of inquiry to the public then delivering on its claim by producing human resources and scholarly works. This combination of people and information has the potential for making useful and valuable things, which some universities are able to patent or otherwise convert into financial support. In other words, science breeds technology. Gatorade™ is a prime example of this scenario. Concocted in the mid-1960s by four University of Florida doctors to combat dehydration among football players, over the next few years, and after various legal adventures, the University of Florida ended up receiving 20% of the revenues from this drink. Keep in mind that Gatorade is little more than water, various salts, flavoring, and sugar (you can read it on the label). The science was not in the discovery of such common substances, but in their mixture, and the financial windfall was produced by business acumen. Doctors mixed up the stuff; football players liked it because it actually seemed to help with dehydration; salesmen named it; attorneys took over; the University of Florida reaps the benefits. None of these events would ever have happened had not (1) dehydration been a problem for all humans doing strenuous physical exercise under certain environmental conditions, (2) somebody sometime asked questions about the blood chemistry of mice, rats, and people, (3) someone somewhere tried to answer those questions; that is, the nerds did their thing: research.

In the above list, (2) is the critical item; formal inquiry as a way of knowing, defined by a discipline and subject, is sustained by curiosity and idealism, the source of questions. As for Gatorade, the history of ideas eventually leading to the first royalty checks probably can be traced back to the 1860s, to Claude Bernard, the Sorbonne physiologist and father of experimental medicine. In a larger sense, *medicine* and *Gatorade* are not the important words; instead, "formal inquiry" is the key to a university's long-term health, financial and otherwise. Institutions that continue to teach this lesson sustain their power and alumni loyalty. Such loyalty, however, most often derives not from the Rumpelstiltskin Moment at halftime on national TV, but from interactions with teachers, teachers who make a difference in some young person's life, open doors, and sweep away the intellectual naïveté that comes naturally with youth. And most often, such teachers are ones who've learned their last big lesson well, and thus embarked—willingly, repeatedly, and on purpose, often dragging others along—on those allegorical journeys during which they develop a deep appreciation for the fundamental nature of inquiry. These teachers know what's important. They also know that what's truly important about higher education cannot be found in textbooks.

When faculty members who actually do and publish research, no matter how seemingly arcane, are sent into the introductory classroom, The Firm's *raison d'être* seeps through those sentences delivered to America's future sitting out there staring back and wishing it had a date instead of an exam. *This is how one approaches a difficult problem*, says the prof whose description of an obscure protozoan has just been accepted for publication in a journal spoken of in rather disparaging terms by some department chair and recently cut from the library to save money; *now listen up!*

The message is clear: approaches to difficult problems usually require a combination of transferable skills not necessarily revealed, or taught, by that $187 textbook. Forget some part of the citric acid cycle? No big deal; look it up using Google. Ignore the transferable skills? Really big deal; you're going to need them a decade from now. Oh, and by the way, a problem's difficulty has absolutely no relationship to its perceived importance. If your grandmother, or your significant other, asks you why you're wasting your time studying *that*, tell her it's the surest way to transform the world into a better place through production of human resources, in this case, an intellectually empowered you. In the long run, it's more important to learn how to learn than to learn—anything.

Our prof doesn't deliver this message in standard English. Instead, he or she teaches the fundamental nature of inquiry by using paralanguage: posture, dress, sequence of sentences, pictures chosen, yes, from that $187 text, tone of voice when responding to questions, and willingness, nowadays, to answer a thousand e-mails a semester. In such a class, for fifty minutes every Monday, Wednesday, and Friday, content— think cell structure and function, or inheritance of flower color in peas—becomes subordinate to the larger lesson: *this is how one approaches a difficult problem.* American business asks for, indeed demands, that The Firm deliver this larger lesson, even as its leaders make out checks to the athletic department. American business, and especially American government, both need, like never before in our history, adaptable people who can work with diverse individuals, who can actually produce something, are globally aware, have analytical habits of mind, have no fear of the unknown (think art, classical music, and science), and share a vital interest in lifelong learning. The nation that buys football tickets doesn't really want what it needs, mainly because when it comes to scholarship, especially in science, all swords are double-edged. So to defuse the fear of science, at least in biology class, we tend to teach what's easily memorized: baby biochemistry, cell biology, Mendelian genetics, and nutrient cycling—the stuff pre-meds believe is important. But if we're organized, and justifiably ornery, and are committed to teaching the needs instead of the wants, we get to evolution. *Here's why evolution is the central unifying theme of life sciences,* says our prof some time during the eleventh week. Out there beyond the auditorium doors, beyond the city streets that separate campus from the real world, someone, an elected official, a big donor, the parents of a star athlete, some writers to the public pulse, are scowling and muttering to themselves: *evolution is a lie, it's just a theory,* not understanding what the word "theory" actually means to a scientist or why "it's just a theory" reveals such a monumental scientific illiteracy.

Our prof continues: *Here's how you recover the past five million years of human, and four billion years of pre-human, history; and, here's how modern molecular techniques are used to actually test hypotheses about evolutionary relationships and patterns of descent.* On the surface all this verbiage sounds like trilobite structure, radio-isotope dating, primate teeth, gene sequencing, and use of cladistic software. What's obvious to any scholar is that this lecture actually concerns inquiry, the nature of evidence, how one infers a history from data, and what kinds of underlying assumptions must be accepted with any methodology. In an engaged prof's class, we experience meta-science, if not meta-education. Our engaged prof is giving these 250 nineteen-year-olds what they need, disguised as content, which is what someone has told them they should want, and thus is delivering The Firm's reason for existence.

Out of the 250 people ostensibly listening to this prof, 125 are wondering why they're being asked to learn the word *trilobite* and cannot envision ever using, or even seeing, that word again. "Trilobite" is not what they've been told, usually by the professional advising system, that they should want or even need to know to gain admission to medical, nursing, or pharmacy school. Another sixty-five or seventy are not hearing "trilobite" or anything else. The rest are writing it down faithfully, suspecting, correctly, that they will indeed see that word again, most likely on an exam. The word itself means nothing; their ability to pick up a strange word, incorporate it into their conversation, and use it sometime in the unforeseen future, in unforeseen circumstances, means everything. "The rest" are getting what they paid for out of American higher education; the word *trilobite* is deposited in their lexicon, and when they withdraw it, unlike their savings and 401k accounts, it will increase in value when taken out and used. The word itself is not education; knowing how to use it, when to use it, and most important why to use it, is what a parent's tuition check should buy.

The diversity of images conjured up by this test question term *trilobite*—although it could as easily have been *Allosaurus* or *Eosimias*—will grow with every visit with their children to a museum, every seventh-page below-the-fold newspaper story about some new fossil discovery, every political debate about climate change, every culture battle over America's three hot-button words: abortion, homosexuality, and evolution. At the lectern, gazing out over this sea of faces, our prof is wondering how to boost the fraction that actually gets it, also known as "the rest." That's his real job at school. He's focusing on the 125 who need to learn a strange word but cannot envision ever using, or even seeing, that word again; they're the group most likely to wake up when faced with an engaged scholar at his or her best. They're also the group most likely to stay asleep, or, for that matter, to simply stay home, when faced with a temporary instructor hired to do grunge duty while a tenured rock star writes his or her ten-million-dollar grant proposal.

I've just described what's happening down in the trenches while up in the bell tower, among the carpeted offices, chancellors and deans look at spreadsheets and wonder how to pay the electric bill. Up in those offices, both the temporary instructor (no health insurance to pay, no obligation to provide laboratory space), and the rock star (overhead dollars into the general fund), look like bargains. But few chancellors or deans ever slip into the back of a large auditorium then silently watch students with their laptops open surfing the web, checking e-mail, connecting with Facebook friends, sometimes checking out porn, or texting friends from all over the country, or all over the world, while up at the podium our bargain is droning on against a backdrop of PowerPoint slides provided by some book publisher and filled with small font text. When it comes to science, especially the teaching of it, bargains are best interpreted in the long view.

◆　　◆　　◆

I'd like to tell you a story about The Firm, but without passing judgment on any of the people, the behaviors, the relationships, or the outcomes involved. What follows is absolutely true, from what I ordered for dinner one evening to what I was doing a few years later at my computer on a morning in April, 2009. The student's name is also true: Shay Hampton; she worked as an undergraduate researcher in my laboratory for a couple of years before graduating in May, 2009. In this regard, she is no different from many others. There has been a long parade of students, both undergraduate and graduate, through our laboratory, and most of them have gone on to very interesting lives. Shay also is good one to talk about in some detail because she exemplifies the human resources that walk into every American university's front door annually by the thousands. In addition, she illustrates the main lesson of research: the allegorical journey that has no direct bearing whatsoever on global human affairs but has every kind of bearing on our intellects, on the traits that drive our global human affairs.

Although she doesn't know it, and wasn't there, Shay's story begins at the Outback Steakhouse in Lincoln, Nebraska, several years ago. Karen and I were seated in a booth, one of those to the left of the bar as you walk in. She ordered a glass of Pinot Grigio and shrimp; I ordered Jack Daniels on the rocks and salmon. We were having a nice conversation, mostly me listening to whatever happened during her day at work, when four suits came in and sat in the booth behind me. There were three good-looking young-ish men and one good looking young-ish woman, all dressed nicely, obviously out-of-town professionals unwinding after an intense day doing something serious. They ordered drinks and proceeded to start talking about the University of Nebraska's Board of Regents. Naturally, I began to listen, and Karen also grew quiet, listening, now watching this group over my shoulder.

From being employed by the University of Nebraska for decades, and being involved in a variety of university assignments, I knew several of the governing board members on a first-name basis. One of them had been my dentist, usually stuffing my mouth full of cotton and clamps before asking how "things were going down at the University." I was still sipping my Jack Daniels when the familiar names started drifting from the suits' booth over into ours. One by one, members of the Board of Regents were being analyzed: their financial situation, their business connections, their voting records on various issues, whether they were conservative (most always are, sometimes seriously so), or liberal (few are, ever), where they lived, and most interestingly, what it would take to talk them into voting on an agenda item to be considered the next day: exclusive vending rights, including all University of Nebraska facilities statewide, at all campuses, and in all athletic venues. The four suits were from Pepsi-Cola. History shows they handled the Board of Regents well and won the contract. You cannot buy Coca-Cola products on our campus now, so like all other employees who so desire, I bring my own to school. But I will never forget that evening at Outback. Now fast-forward a few years to the student named Shay Hampton.

In one of the more farsighted actions my institution has carried out over the four-plus decades of my employment there, someone in the upper administration squeezed money out of Pepsi to support undergraduate research as part of the exclusive vending rights deal. The program is officially called UCARE (Undergraduate Creative and Research Experience), and through brief proposals, UNL students can apply for small grants to support their independent study under a faculty member's tutelage. Thus Shay joined a small group of undergraduates working in my lab, taking advantage of Pepsi's "generosity." When student research is involved, especially undergraduate research, I always try to match personalities and material. Shay was not much different from other undergrads in the sense that she had many obligations, some of them conflicting, and all of them functioning to make time management her daily challenge. Nor was she different from our other undergraduate researchers in another respect: her project was to concern the biology of gregarines, obscure one-celled organisms that live mainly in the gut of insects and other invertebrates. We talked about various projects that might be done with these parasites. Many years ago, when it became obvious that undergraduates wanting to do research were to become a regular part of my professional life, I asked the question: how can undergraduates accomplish a true scientific exploration, given the demands on their lives, the time constraints, and the issue of money? The key to mentoring success in this case is possession; the student, not the prof, has to own his or her project. What are the easiest, most economical, legitimate research projects for a twenty-year-old student to actually own? What can a college junior do in the next two years that accomplishes the same thing a faculty member has to do in those same two years: publish an original paper, a contribution to what's called "the primary literature"? And finally, what question can this junior in college address that demands he or she take on all the logistical burdens of research that comes along with ownership—everything from washing glassware to maintaining cultures to statistical analysis? Many years ago I answered those questions in the most effective and economical way I could imagine: work on the most common, most diverse, most cooperative, and most beautiful of all parasites, the gregarines.

Let's begin with personality. Shay Hampton appeared on the roster of my Field Parasitology class, BIOS 487, during the summer between her freshman and sophomore year, at the Cedar Point Biological Station (CPBS) north of Ogallala, Nebraska. To quote from the several hundred letters of recommendation I've written for former CPBS students: "Field Parasitology at CPBS is a very demanding course that requires laboratory and field exercises, a collection, daily exams, daily written assignments, an independent research project, and regular oral and written presentations. In addition, CPBS is an in-residence program, so we do get to know the students very well and watch them interact with their fellow students." Shay's appearance in this class was unusual, especially without being personally recruited by me because of previous classroom performance. She'd obviously made a decision to stretch out, intellectually, and seek a challenge not many of her cohorts would welcome. She'd also obviously acted counter to advice commonly dished out by professional advisers, who typically tell students to "wait until you're ready for this challenge," whatever "ready" means to people like professional advisers who have never been to a field program. Her appearance in Cedar Point's Goodall Lodge on the Sunday evening prior to the start of classes is thus a key to her personality: she's not afraid of much. In fact, after watching her work for two years, I'd say she's probably not afraid of anything.

At Cedar Point, Shay jumped on a class project involving gregarine parasites of damselflies. I say "jumped on" because the first day of class we'd done an exercise with these parasites as an excuse to learn entomology, dissection and measurement techniques, identification (both of the parasites and their insect hosts), spreadsheet design, data analysis, and presentation, all in the space of fourteen hours. Shay and her partner, Kacie Meyers, another fearless first-year student, immediately picked up on a number of interesting questions that could be addressed using the numerical information provided by this host-parasite system. Where most students saw something they needed to learn, Shay and her partner saw something that gave them the power to conduct a formal inquiry, something to *do*, which in the doing would give them transferable skills. Three weeks later Shay and Kacie stood up in front of the class to present their results and data interpretation, conceding, in the process, that we were pretending to hold a real scientific society meeting by role-playing. They'd worked hard on their PowerPoint images, the sequence of statements and ideas, the rationale behind their project, the hypotheses to be tested, the methods, the data, and finally, their conclusions about what it all meant. Now it was time to put on a show, and they knew it.

Was Shay a "real" scientist after only three weeks in the field? I answer the question "yes," although many, if not most, of my colleagues would claim "no." Why the difference of opinion? My answer to this question is: when a sequence of mental acts characterizes your approach to a problem, no matter how seemingly trivial that problem, then you have become defined by the discipline. When you begin thinking like an historian then you've stepped over the line that separates historians from non-historians, perhaps not very far over the line, but over, nevertheless. The same statement can be made about the line between artists and non-artists, musicians and non-musicians, and scientists and non-scientists. Once this mental transformation occurs, the rest is easy. Why might my colleagues deny such assertions? I don't know the answer to that question, but I do know that the Shay Hamptons of the world tend to walk into my lab and not theirs, as the real Shay Hampton did a few weeks after her summer's Cedar Point experience.

I was sitting at my microscope doing some biology; I don't know exactly what kind of biology, but most of mine involves microscopes (see chapter 4, "Through a Lens"). Shay came in, sat down at the table across from me, and said:

"May I work in your lab?"

Usually when I get asked such questions, by such students, I try to remain relatively calm and professorly rather than jump up and down screaming "YES!!" That simple question— *May I work in your lab?*—is the ultimate reward of a scientist. Nor do I remember why we settled on the particular insects she decided to study for the next two years, except that we had these two beetle species growing in culture, and no one had looked at their parasites, at least not with a great deal of care. Unexplored territory is a powerful lure, and not just for the Roy Chapman Andrews' of the world; college sophomores like Shay also tend to be fascinated with the unknown, even if the wilderness is inside an insect instead of out on the Gobi Desert. Furthermore, the beetles we were rearing—*Cryptolestes pusillus* and *Latheticus oryzae*—are notorious stored products pests. There is an outside chance you've eaten some of these insects, or their parts, because they infest flour, cereals, and grains around the world, and cereal grain products, especially if stored for any length of time, are rarely free of insects and mites. The beetles' scientific names reflect their physical stature and secret lives: *crypto-* means "hidden," *pusillus* means "very small," and *oryzae* refers to rice. If crawling upon a dime, one adult *Cryptolestes pusillus* could sit easily on the tip of Franklin Roosevelt's nose and an adult *Latheticus oryzae* could fit in his ear with plenty of room to spare.

The ultimate problem with hosts and parasites is a co-evolutionary one, an explanation of why certain parasites occur in certain hosts. This problem is found throughout areas such as human and veterinary medicine, disease ecology, global movement of pathogens, diagnosis and diagnostic techniques, immunology and vaccine development, and budgetary planning for disease control. The terms *swine flu* and *bird flu*, for example, reveal the movement of infectious agents into places—a human's respiratory system, for example—where they did not originally evolve.

Shay's project thus was a small model of a very large phenomenon. Her material came in the form of two small plastic jars containing whole wheat flour, wheat germ, wheat bran, and yeast, all in magic proportions, and ... beetles living happily and reproducing like crazy. Each jar was a simple model for an economy with a public health problem: organisms, most of which were infected, seeking and finding nutritional needs, perhaps competing with one another for mates, reproducing, and eventually dying. In the lab, *C. pusillus* and *L. oryzae* (whose Latin names are certainly no odder than names in the Lincoln, Nebraska, telephone book!) were separated, but in nature they could, and probably should, occur together. So Shay's simple question became: do these stored grain pests share parasite species, and if not, why not? But before she could do anything else with the parasites in these insects, she still had to answer biology's most pervasive and enduring question: *What is it?*

This question, of course, refers to the beetles' parasites. If you can't distinguish letter X from letter Y, then you don't know whether they occur in the same word. If you can't distinguish Parasite A from Parasite B, then you can never answer fundamental questions such as: are they restricted to their respective host species or can they invade other host species? The problem of cross-infection is a fairly important one, and not just for influenza virus. For example, a roundworm named *Baylisascaris procyonis*, that occurs naturally in raccoons, can invade humans, especially young children, and end up in the nervous system, causing severe meningoencephalitis and subsequent neurological disorders. Cats, including family pets, can harbor *Toxoplasma gondii*, a protozoan capable of invading fetal nervous systems, resulting in tragic and fatal hydrocephaly in newborn infants. And the last time you went to the blood bank as a donor, you were asked whether you had Chagas' disease, caused by a notorious zoonotic parasite, a flagellate sustained largely in wild mammals throughout much of Latin America but that easily infects humans who are bitten by the carriers, which are large blood-sucking insects ("kissing bugs").

So Shay decided to ask this same question about her model system consisting of two tiny beetle species: can their parasites infect the opposite hosts, and if not, why not? But first, as always in unexplored regions, whether they are the Gobi Desert or insect intestines, we must solve the problem of what we've actually discovered. In Shay's case, the discovery was of two kinds of truly beautiful and mysterious cell-organisms, both unknown to science. She was thus faced with a task that has challenged all biological explorers from Aristotle, Linnaeus, and Darwin to modern explorers, deep in tropical jungles trying to discover exactly what it is we Third Millennium humans are destroying at a mass-extinction rate. This task is, on the surface, a simple one: describe what you've found. But in practice the task is anything but simple. Indeed, the description of an hitherto unknown species is one of the most highly educational of all biologists' options, primarily because the word "description" is a technical one, meaning a published paper that fulfills stringent criteria of measurement, illustration, and justification, and also passes anonymous peer review.

After two years of measurement, making permanent slides, analyzing digital images, collecting beetles feces for cysts, experimenting with methods for ensuring cysts actually developed into "spores" whose structure she needed for her formal description, digging into the depths of ancient and arcane literature, much of it in foreign languages, studying the electron microscope screen for the perfect images, and talking constantly with her lab mates about the criteria for distinguishing species, Shay finally pulled a piece of antique equipment from a drawer and attached it to a microscope. This equipment was a camera lucida, a device that splits a light beam and allows you to trace an image with your pencil, even though that image is of a structurally complex cell 1/3000 of an inch long. Wikipedia's contributor on the subject claims "The camera lucida is still available today through art-supply channels, but is not well known or widely used." In this case Wikipedia's authors are right on target: camera lucidas are often considered antiques, and some of the ones in our lab certainly are. But they are essential instruments for describing nature because they allow a person to draw pictures that have the correct proportions. Those pictures, with structural details you cannot capture with a photograph, are essential features of any new species description.

Thus Shay learned the pleasures of working with a camera lucida, the challenge of making large-scale ink drawings, and the satisfaction of arranging those drawings into a plate worthy of publication. Then to fulfill her obligations to Pepsi, she took all the information from her two years worth of labor: all the methods, hundreds of measurements, data and statistical analysis, digital photomicrographs, electron micrographs, others' published descriptions (often decades old and in obscure journals), information about the beetles, rationale for doing the project, and conclusions, and made a poster for presentation at a scientific meeting. "Made a poster" is code for "now, instead of a scientist, you're a marketing and PR person." Shay Hampton's intellectual journey may have started with the most pervasive and enduring question in biology—What is it?—but as is the case with all scientists, her journey ended with a writer's and artist's dilemma: tell a true story, to a public that knows nothing, and probably cares nothing, about your subject, through the use of skillfully, and thoughtfully, assembled words and pictures, and tell that story in a way that makes the public understand, and appreciate, what you've accomplished.

Shay Hampton's poster is now tacked to the wall across from my laboratory door. Every day I look at it and am reminded of The Firm's essential lesson: years of intellectual endeavor end with a seemingly minor accomplishment that can be buried in an obscure journal or summarized on a 30" × 48" sheet of slick-finished paper. But the real product of this endeavor walks away to a summer job, carrying the experience in her brain. The reputation mongers look at Shay's poster and think: hmmm, just another species description. Why hasn't she cured cancer? The answer to that last questions is: well some day she might; but for the moment, she's a walking, talking, example of The Firm's *raison d'être:* that allegorical journey during which one develops a deep appreciation for the fundamental nature of inquiry. And even though she was an undergraduate, her basic experience is the same as that lived by every scholar, including every faculty member, no matter the discipline, no matter how much money is involved, or how much technology, who embarks on that allegorical journey.

◆　　◆　　◆

If I didn't finish a chapter entitled "The Firm" with some dirty laundry, every reader with university connections would snicker and accuse me of gutlessness, without knowing, of course, that I had a mother who always considered metaphorical dirty laundry beneath her dignity, and that I currently have a wife who clearly thinks the same way. Both of these elegant ladies function(ed) to keep most of my baser instincts in check, and usually at least somewhat successfully, over the past seven decades. Nevertheless, campus politics are simply too much fun to avoid altogether. In addition, no chapter about The Firm would be complete without some dirt. I promise that I'll do my very best to disguise the individuals involved, although this task may be quite a literary challenge. If I'm successful, then every reader who's ever worked for any university anywhere will instantly put names on these ethereal characters, and even though the names will stick, sometimes tightly, they will vary depending on the time and place.

In 2008, I published a book entitled *Outwitting College Professors*, and asked that my freshman biology students read it. About a third the way through the fall semester, a student named Paige Ahart walked into my office with her copy of *OCP*, and her most recent writing assignment, wanting to talk about both. At the time, Paige was the only student in the previous ten years—that is, she was one out of about three thousand—who had asked that I review his or her writing and talk seriously about narrative structure and techniques. Admittedly, she may have been taking some advice found in OCP, but the fact that she was the only one, *the only one out of three thousand over a period of ten years* who had taken me up on an offer of help, meant that she was a marked individual. She also wrote beautifully. So when I needed a reader who was completely unfamiliar with either me or the material in this *Pieces of the Plains* manuscript, I e-mailed Paige and she agreed to be that reader. Now she was not only one out of three thousand, but also someone whose work a faculty member would actually know well enough to write a meaningful letter of recommendation two or three years hence. On that first visit, she wanted to talk about *Outwitting College Professors.*

"Are there really people like that?" she asked, referring to a section, about faculty members, headed DANGEROUS TYPES; BE ALERT AND BE AWARE.

"Yes," I answered.

"Here?"

"Yes," I answered. A ghost of my mother appeared at the door, warning me to back away from this discussion. So I continued in a highly generalized way about the behavior of people who work in systems where the currency is reputation. Paige seemed satisfied, but also uneasy, so we turned to her own essay about some campus plant.

Remember that someone who has been on any university's faculty for forty-three years has experienced quite a bit of the business, served on lots of committees, reviewed lots of faculty records, done some administrative duties, and encountered thousands, if not tens of thousands, of people, ranging from those in deep trouble to a few in positions of extreme power regardless of their titles. During those forty-three years of employment by The Firm, I've been asked by an administrator to save all correspondence from a fellow faculty member because a case for denial of tenure couldn't be made on the basis of research and teaching, so it needed to be made on the basis of personality ("_____ is a bad colleague."); warned by an outside program review team member to keep my mouth shut around certain administrators; and told to retrieve lab notebooks from a long-departed graduate student so that an administrator could demonstrate the student's adviser was lying about when a certain project was started (the adviser turned out to be telling the truth and the published paper was, after all, counted for promotion).

I've seen highly qualified senior faculty members volunteer—numerous times, in writing—to teach very challenging, large-enrollment, freshman classes, and to help younger faculty members master the art of dealing with such intimidating instructional settings, only to have their offer ignored completely—and repeatedly—by administrators. At stake was instructional quality for two or three thousand students, in this case majors headed mostly for the health professions. The kindest interpretation of this human resource management behavior is that it was a product of unforgivable administrator ignorance about the discipline. The next kindest interpretation is that the administrator involved didn't want the faculty member in contact with the department's majors, probably because of jealousy or psychological insecurity about another teacher's reputation for classroom performance. In terms of kindness, further interpretations drop off pretty sharply.

I've chaired a committee formed to hear a formal complaint, by a faculty member, against administrators for acting correctly and in accordance with the Regents' bylaws, our official governance document; been on search committees that voted for candidates on the basis of area of expertise, in the process purposefully ignoring, or not recognizing, evidence for other candidates' obvious skills that were critically needed by a department; been on search committees that disregarded, repeatedly, compelling evidence for total lack of interpersonal skills in candidates, thus complete lack of human resource management skills, and recommended hiring of administrative candidates who turned out to be complete failures; and had extremely stressful encounters with pathological control freaks, watched other faculty members struggle with similar situations in other departments, and seen faculty careers flourish under administrators who were so hands-off that one wondered why they got paid an administrative stipend. Such administrators were obviously following the Carnegie rules for success: surround yourself with good people, get out of their way and let them do their job, then go brag about their performance.

This dirt discussion could go on for a couple of more chapters, but what you've read is a pretty representative sample. Obviously my graduate students hear it all. I want them educated, not surprised, when they encounter these kinds of situations years hence in their own academic careers—and they will. We usually have plenty to talk about, so much so that eventually their eyes start to glaze over and they go back to their research.

Dirt is frustrating, of course, but there are equally powerful ameliorating forces in higher education, namely, idealism and the several thousand young people who walk into your front door annually. As a result of being a parasitologist, attending parasitology and tropical medicine meetings, being co-author of four editions of *Foundations of Parasitology*, thus reading thousands of papers about infectious disease, watching my nation embark on ill-advised, and sometimes downright stupid, military adventures, and reading—constantly reading: history, religion, economics, anthropology, sociology—I've come to the conclusion that anyone who is a tenured faculty member at a large American university is living in the upper 5%, maybe upper 1%, of all humanity throughout all history in terms of health, intellectual and personal freedom, economic stability, social and cultural richness, and personal safety.

In my opinion, this last statement should be the opening lines of any advertisement for a faculty or administrative position in American academia: *Anyone who is a tenured faculty member at a large American university is living in the upper 5%, maybe upper 1%, of all humanity throughout all history in terms of health, intellectual and personal freedom, economic stability, social and cultural richness, and personal safety.* Perhaps the second statement should be: *Your nation's finest young people are going to show up at your front door every August by the thousands; now make sure they walk out of here four years hence understanding exactly what a privilege it is to be living in this nation, with this constitution, and this division of powers among the legislative, executive, and judicial branches.* I know it's too much to demand that the third sentence be something like *now turn off Rush Limbaugh,* but it's not too much of an expectation that whatever educational experience is delivered by The Firm, the result will be the same.

PART III

A Future

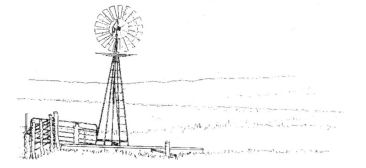

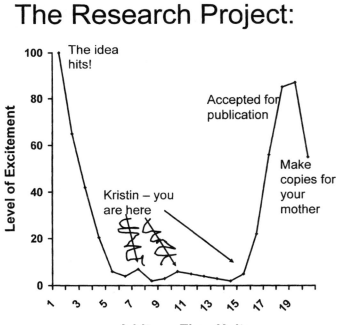

What is Science?

The most productive scientists, installed in million-dollar laboratories, have no time to think about the big picture and see little profit in it ... It is therefore not surprising to find physicists who do not know what a gene is, and biologists who guess that string theory has something do to with violins.

—E. O. Wilson, *Consilience*

Science is a formalized study of nature, with the intent of discovering mechanisms that produce, maintain, and control natural phenomena. The term "natural phenomena" can include everything from the origin of galaxies to mating behavior of squid, or anything between any other two examples of the extreme and arcane. Not all natural phenomena are so strange, however; many of them are quite familiar, for example, infectious diseases (chicken pox, mumps, common cold, AIDS), hurricanes, earthquakes, and the birth of human babies. Some of these natural phenomena are of great interest to us because of personal, political, or financial reasons; others simply stir up curiosity or appeal to our aesthetic sense, e.g., shenanigans of backyard squirrels and a magnificent sunset. But regardless of our personal interest in a natural phenomenon, or lack thereof, some scientist probably has studied that same phenomenon with an eye toward explaining its origin, developmental processes, and the forces that control it. Science is therefore a way of knowing, but unlike other ways of knowing, science actually produces something, namely, technology, that can, with proper refinement or development, be used to control part of nature.

Science is not the same as technology, although science uses technology in its exploration of the universe from distant galactic clusters to molecular events deep within a cell. Conversely, people who seek to develop technology usually rely on scientific discoveries. Thus the two areas complement and enable one another. Technology is to science as hammers, saws, and squares are to carpentry; you can't do the latter without using the former, but you can possess the former with no ability or intent to do the latter. Hammers, saws, and squares don't make a person an accomplished carpenter any more than a microscope and DNA sequencing machine make someone an accomplished scientist. Science is an activity in which *people* (scientists) use *devices* (technology) to explore the natural world. When such exploration produces something that solves a problem (defined by *humans*), then we are grateful and have a positive feeling about the science, a good example being the technology of vaccination against smallpox or polio. But when exploration produces a vision of the universe that we don't particular want to hear about, we sometimes have a negative feeling about the science involved, good examples being Galileo's explanations of planetary movements and, of course, the emergence of humans during the past several million years of vertebrate evolution.

Thus science is easily, if not best, described by that tired old metaphor of a two-edged sword: it gives you power but it can also hurt you. It can give you happiness, but it can make you angry and frustrated. In this encounter with the two sharp edges, it is well to remember the difference between science and technology, and to remember that both are *human* activities. Humans have a way of producing things that seem to take on lives of their own, large government agencies are an outstanding example. Science is certainly one of these things, although the world's scientific enterprise is much larger, more diffuse, and less controllable than even the Social Security Administration or the Department of Defense. Science is so extensive and diffuse because, probably much like religion, it is based on a fundamental human characteristic—curiosity— and most probably, curiosity derived from both consciousness and wonder.

We often describe non-human animals, especially our pets, as being curious, but we have no idea whether such apparent curiosity is based in wonder. Nor do we know whether other species are conscious in the same sense we are aware of ourselves and of the deeper meanings and symbolism in our environments. Many humans, especially in developed nations, will argue that their dogs and cats are "almost human" and in the worst case scenario people and pets come to look like one another, especially if both live long enough. But pets are not people, and just because we like to hang that baggage on them, our skewed view of their fundamental biology doesn't alter their genetic makeup very much no matter how successful they are at teaching us when to feed and pet them. I was discussing this issue one day with a colleague who used his girlfriend's schnauzer as an example.

"This dog's lying there on the floor asleep and lets out a big fart," says my friend. "Then he suddenly wakes up and starts chasing his own fart and barking at it." Such behavior was cited as evidence that this particular pooch had so little self-awareness that it was not able to distinguish his own combination of methane and sulfur dioxide emissions from those possibly produced by a rival. I'm not sure that this particular schnauzer's behavior was typical of all dogs, but the case certainly illustrated the extent to which the pet's owner and guest were people, aware of cause and effect, and willing to pass judgment on another species' traits. If that schnauzer were a scientist, he probably would be curious about why that gas smelled so bad, and thinking way ahead to a whole lot of neurobiology experiments to trace the responses of certain kinds of nerve endings to chemical compounds diffusing through the atmosphere, all resulting in socially aggressive behavior toward an imagined intruder. Maybe in the back of this scientist's mind is the idea that perhaps such research might eventually lead to the ultimate aphrodisiac. This difference between the schnauzer's and the imaginary scientist's respective reactions to a natural phenomenon illustrates clearly the roles of wonder and curiosity as stimulants to research.

Science thrives on a combination of curiosity and ideas, and without this combination science becomes relatively boring and unproductive. Indeed, many scientists will tell you that the idea stage is the most exciting part of any research project, a stage that often happens in strange places and at unexpected times—driving down the highway, in a bar with friends, waking up in the middle of the night, or even sitting in church listening to a parable that sends one's mind wandering. The first data also produce quite a bit of excitement, mainly because they show that your chosen research methods actually work. Then the real labor begins: weeks, months, sometimes years of repetition, data analysis, manuscript preparation, and all the time, additional and competing ideas are generating excitement you don't have the time to pursue—just yet. Excitement starts returning once a manuscript nears completion; a true adrenaline rush can occur when a research paper is submitted electronically, that "Enter" key is pressed, and you know that those months or years of work, all aimed at testing your exciting idea, are now subject to anonymous peer review.

By the time the thing appears in print, you're usually pursuing new ideas, the ones that produced all the excitement while you were repeating all those experiments over and over again. But closure is as essential to science as curiosity. That publication, the one you send to your proud mother, is like the song in the second verse of Henry Wadsworth Longfellow's famous poem that this same mother probably read to you as a child (*I Shot an Arrow into the Air*): it ends up in the heart of a friend, or in the mind of some stranger half a world a way, a fellow scientist excited by ideas, including the ideas your own research has generated. Thus the excitement of research, and of the scientific career, is sustained, and a nation has its needed supply of scientific expertise.

Regardless of how exciting science may be to the scientist, it sometimes gets a bum rap from a lot of people for being boring and difficult to understand, if not outright unpleasant. If you talk to enough people about science, especially at social occasions, you routinely hear the expression "I'm just not good at science." This declaration could mean anything from "I'm just being polite by not telling you [a scientist] that

I think science is evil and only really despicable people become scientists" to "I made a D in biology as a freshman and have never forgiven my teacher or adviser even though that happened thirty years ago." But the phrase "I'm just not *good* at science" often really means "I'm not the least bit *interested* in science unless, of course, it involves matters that affect *me or my family right now.*" These matters can be almost anything you read in the newspaper or see on television, but they typically involve politics, money, or health.

For example, a low-level nuclear waste facility, planned for your county, turns even grandmothers into amateur nuclear physicists. A childhood behavioral disorder diagnosis turns a young mother into a medical researcher as quickly as she can get to the computer and call up Google. And a perceived threat to someone's religious beliefs can easily transform that person into a philosopher of science, determined to eliminate mention of evolution from local public school curricula, even though that individual may not be able to tell a Mississippian ostracod fossil from a Devonian foraminiferan. (Ostracods are tiny, often microscopic, crustaceans, and foraminiferans are amebas with wondrously complex and structurally diverse skeletons. Both have extensive and well-documented evolutionary histories, but when evolution is mentioned in the culture wars, the warriors are rarely if ever talking about ostracods or foraminiferans.)

Of course these three individuals are not *really* nuclear physicists, medical researchers, or philosophers of science respectively; they just think they are, and believe they are behaving in a manner consistent with the behavior of their models. And in truth they are behaving like scientists, although not nearly as effectively, and with only a tiny fraction of the resulting knowledge and understanding that a professional scientist would obtain by using "primary literature," that is, published scientific research papers. Furthermore, the local citizens' study is likely to be guided by personal or political goals: to stop the building of this nuclear waste facility, to help physicians treat the child, and to change whatever is being taught in public schools.

The scientist's study, on the other hand, is most likely guided by curiosity or a desire to build, or maintain, a reputation because respect for one's opinion is the currency in science. If the nuclear waste facility is built because a real scientist has demonstrated, convincingly, that it poses no threat to people or wildlife, then that scientist has bragging rights. If the nuclear waste facility is not built because another scientist can demonstrate, convincingly, that its design is flawed and that the leakage will indeed be a public health hazard, then that scientist also has bragging rights. A year after the political decision, locals may be sighing in relief or still seething with bitter anger, but there's a pretty good chance the scientist is off somewhere else bragging about his/her role in the process and working on another project.

In culture wars in which science is a participant, as is the case with evolution in the United States today, it often seems as if the true battle is being fought over thought processes and mindsets. The question—Do you believe in evolution?—asked by reporters of American presidential candidates during a so-called debate during 2007, serves to illustrate this kind of battle. Belief is a human trait that doesn't necessarily have anything to do with fact, except that belief typically drives actions. In other words, we can believe something whether that something is true or not, or even based in reality, then act on such a belief. We might believe that we *will* win the lottery, for example, although such belief is based on infinitesimal odds, indeed, on odds so small that they approach zero. On the other hand, we also believe that we can win the lottery, and in this case the belief is well-founded because of two reasons: first, however infinitesimal, the odds are not in fact zero, and second, somebody actually does win periodically, demonstrating the inevitability of a winner that could just as easily have been one of us losers. If we truly understand what it means to believe something, then we also understand the difference between *will* and *can* and this understanding probably increases the ornery pleasure we get from buying a ticket and imagining what we would do with all that money, knowing all the time that such mental entertainment is worth far more than $1 regardless of the ultimate outcome of this week's drawing.

Evolution, on the other hand, unlike the lottery, is a realm of scientific inquiry, a process that has been demonstrated time and time again to work, and a theory. One does not "believe" in realms of scientific inquiry, processes, and theories. Instead, inquiry about process, using theory as a guide, provides a particular path toward understanding the process. To a scientist "Do you believe in evolution?" is a pretty stupid question, although to a politician, or a reporter looking for political sparks, it is a great question. This difference in quality of the same question residing in different people's minds is derived from the respective mindsets of reporters, politicians, and scientists. We believe that we understand politicians' and reporters' mindsets: the former wants to win and will do or say about anything it takes to influence voters, and the latter wants a good story, preferably by deadline. If our belief about politicians and reporters is somewhat correct, then their behavior is more or less consistent with "fact," or with observation, although routinely shaded by impression.

But it is almost impossible to understand the scientific mind without also understanding the fundamental structure of scientific inquiry, structure being defined as the components of a system and the interactions between such components. Scientific inquiry is built upon observations, ideas, and approaches to problem solving, all human endeavors. This structure—the presence of and interactions between observation, thoughts, and approaches—helps explain why science itself is a distinctly human trait, certainly as distinctively human as religion. Chimpanzees, our closest non-human relatives, may explore their immediate environments, but their techniques and approaches are not at all what we would call "science." Chimpanzees make observations, remember whatever they have seen, sometimes act on their experiences and memories, and can pass along some learned behaviors, sometimes unintentionally. But they don't do science. Insofar as we know, they don't formulate hypotheses, don't do statistical analysis, don't use mathematics, don't publish in journals, and don't design experiments. Nor do chimpanzees assimilate observations and infer causality, developing real theories the way scientists such as astronomers do. In all fairness to chimps, they are a long way from what we would call "dumb" and they exhibit some exceedingly human-like traits such as emotions, quasi-politics, duplicity, and competition. But chimps don't do real science. Or, to phrase it more accurately, we have never observed them doing what we would call real science, or if we did, we didn't understand what the chimps were doing.

Science as it is typically taught in public schools, and as usually presented to the public, is mostly what we would call "proximal" or "normal" science because it is based on questions that begin with the word *how*. An example of such a question might be "How is sugar broken down into energy, water, and carbon dioxide?" This question is an important one, obviously, because it concerns fundamental metabolic processes that our bodies use continuously and without which there would certainly be no human life as we know it today. Similarly, one might ask "How is the sun's energy captured by living organisms?" This question is an important one, too, perhaps more important than the one about sugar metabolism, because if life could not capture the sun's radiant energy then there would be no life at all as we know it—no cereal grains, no olives, no potatoes, no domestic livestock, no chimpanzees, no tropical forests, and no coral reefs. But both of these questions are ones addressing function, and both have been answered by chemists who study reactions between molecules. Also, both of these questions begin with the word *how*.

In the case of proximal ("how") questions, we can usually "prove" an answer, especially in those cases where we can provide ourselves with material to repeat experiments. We can grow corn seedlings by the millions if necessary, grind them up into cytoplasmic soup, and carry out chemical studies on their metabolic processes over and over again. We can manipulate these corn plants genetically by skillful, indeed Darwinian, breeding and selection, and by doing so eventually associate chemical properties with inherited variations. We are able, by formulating insightful hypotheses, and doing laboratory studies on our abundant and cooperative material, to demonstrate clearly that corn seedlings carry out a series of chemical reactions leading to the capture of radiant energy. Thus we can prove something happens regularly and such proof usually satisfies a critical public.

The kind of science I have just described also is what Thomas Kuhn (*The Structure of Scientific Revolutions*) would call "normal science" in the sense that it addresses accepted questions, ones that the scientific community itself considers important and legitimate. We know plants capture the sun's energy (photosynthesis), and we know that we depend on plants for food because of that ability to capture energy, so the processes by which this capture takes place are legitimate ones for serious study. Maybe if we know enough about those processes, we can improve upon them, or use them for some other purpose such as making ethyl alcohol to fuel our automobiles. Thus everyone, including both scientists and nonscientists, can readily agree that the question of how plants capture the sun's energy is a legitimate one that scientists need to be studying. We also agree that the methods of studying this process are applicable to such research, and that any new methods that we develop can be adequately tested to determine if they, too, are appropriate tools for studying the processes of photosynthesis.

Instead of asking how corn plants trap the sun's radiant energy, we also could ask "How can corn plants get dates to the prom?" That question is not a legitimate one for a variety of reasons. But before we ridicule someone who asks how corn plants get dates to the prom, we should remember that it has not been too many years since questions about genetic engineering were not legitimate ones, either. Many manipulations carried out routinely today by molecular biologists would have been considered science fiction at best, if not outright fantasy, a generation ago. In addition, if you go to enough scientific lectures, there is an excellent chance you will hear someone use the phrase "date to the prom" in a metaphorical way to describe successful mating events between organisms, for example tapeworms, that have never heard of a prom and are never likely to be at one, either, except by accident in the gut of some chaperone. Thus farmers plant corn in rectangular plots in part because the plants are wind-pollinated grasses and so square-ish fields maximize attendance at the prom, metaphorically speaking, although I'm not sure many of those same farmers, watching their own daughters heading out to the senior prom in a nearby town, would be comfortable with the full implications of the scientists' metaphor.

In contrast to asking how corn plants trap energy, if we ask "why" corn seedlings eventually produce corn seeds, we suddenly have a question that is unanswerable except in evolutionary terms, a question of origin, or an *ultimate* question instead of a *proximal*—functional—one that begins with "how." Public school and televised science do quite well with proximal questions but they fail miserably at ultimate questions. The reason they fail is because they do not address the nature of evidence, the process of inference from comparative observations, and the testing of historical hypotheses. These three subjects are fairly sophisticated ones for both school children and the general public, and indeed for many scientists. There is not much evidence that the general public even cares why corn plants produce corn seeds, caring only *whether* they produce seeds, and in what volume. There is even less evidence that the general public cares about why different grass species have distinctive flower structures, or why wind-pollinated grasses have such different flowers than insect-pollinated orchids. Yet it is the "why" question that sustains our culture war over evolution, still boiling in the very geographical heart of America: Kansas.

When scientists seek answers to "why" questions, answers that do not involve supernatural forces—for example, an intelligent designer—then those scientists seem to be encroaching on a realm of intellectual and spiritual life that historically has been controlled by the religious establishment. We all know, from our study of history, what happens when science confronts a religious establishment, especially one with considerable political power. In one of the most familiar cases from history, Galileo was sent before the Inquisition and imprisoned for championing the idea that the Earth revolved around the sun and not vice versa. Although today that condemnation and imprisonment would seem outright ridiculous, especially for publishing material claiming the Earth orbits the sun, remember that in the 1500s the geocentric universe was a product of extreme ignorance. Thus the real issue in our current cultural wars is not whether "evolution is a fact," but whether ignorance fuels a controversy with serious political overtones, especially in a heavily armed nation that is technology dependent and losing economic ground daily to more secular societies such as China.

Galileo's troubles resulted from a political system in which belief trumped evidence, indeed, in which belief was taken to be evidence. There is certainly nothing in the historical record that suggests contemporary individuals or even modern societies are immune to troubles arising from this same situation, namely, belief trumping, if not being taken as, evidence. Perhaps the best documented example of such trouble is the fate of New Orleans at the hands of Hurricane Katrina in 2005. Katrina was the most destructive and costly such storm in United States history, and much of the destruction, estimated at over $80 billion worth, and the loss of nearly two thousand lives, can be attributed to erosion of coastal wetlands and inadequacy of protective levees. Scientists had warned for years that this kind of disaster was inevitable, and explained why, such explanation being founded on clear understanding of coastal ecology and global meteorology (see the cover story of the October, 2001, issue of *Scientific American*).

Of course politicians ignored such warning, and just as of course, the reason was scientific illiteracy and inability to explain, to a taxpaying public, why massive expenditures would be necessary (for levee construction), why coastal development magnified the danger (loss of natural buffer zones), and why the really important question was not whether a Katrina-level storm would hit, along with the attendant damage and loss of life, but *when* it would hit. Science, as a discipline, remember, focuses on evidence; in this case there was substantial evidence to support scientists' predictions, enough evidence, in fact, for the scientific community to consider New Orleans somewhat of an historical "experiment."

Historical experiments are a little bit like so-called "natural experiments" in the sense that scientists predict some results, then people in general watch while nature does something to test this prediction. In science, belief results from a negotiable interpretation of evidence. We believe that a statement about nature is true until it is demonstrated otherwise through the use of observation and appropriate evidence, such evidence sometimes arising through observation of a "natural experiment." In the case of Katrina, one obvious null hypothesis to be tested was: *there is no difference between tropical storms.* In this case, nature performed in a way that provided appropriate evidence and that hypothesis was rejected. As an aside, several million residents of Florida, Georgia, Alabama, Mississippi, Louisiana, and Texas also could have told their political leaders that the null hypothesis had already been rejected by the time Katrina landed.

The scientific description of this historical experiment is almost clinical—"That hypothesis was rejected."—but the human and economic aftermath of any decades-long experiment involving people's lives is an ongoing sad lesson about the social impact of scientific illiteracy by people in major positions of power and responsibility. No candidate for public office should ever be expected to have scientific knowledge equal to that of a professional scientist. Every candidate for public office should be expected to understand why scientific evidence is important to society, why in the long term ideology never trumps nature, and why he or she should be articulate enough to explain, honestly, the same way a scientist would be forced to by anonymous peer reviewers, why belief about how nature behaves should never drive public policy when it is obvious that such belief is ill-founded and not supported by observations. There are plenty of situations in which it's okay to act dumb; we pay money to see entertainers do that. But there also are plenty of situations in which it is dangerous and stupid to act dumb; we should be voting so that we don't have to witness scientific illiteracy in elected office, or, like the people in New Orleans' Ninth Ward, to live with the results.

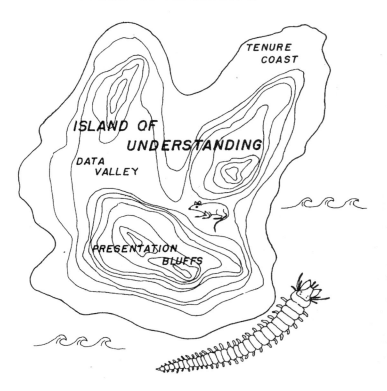

SEA OF IGNORANCE

TENURE
COAST

ISLAND OF
UNDERSTANDING

DATA
VALLEY

PRESENTATION
BLUFFS

Why are Politicians so Scientifically Illiterate?

A United States policy that could find no other option, he suggested, was one of "indolent short-term expediency."

—Barbara Tuchman, *Stillwell and the American Experience in China, 1911–1945*

Elected officials tend to be scientifically illiterate for two reasons: first, often they are either businessmen or attorneys, and neither of these professions requires or encourages scientific literacy; and, second, real scientists and serious teachers, those who are most likely to be quite literate, typically have neither the taste for, nor the resources to seek, elected public office. In a pluralistic society such as ours, both reasons are fairly legitimate. The business community's scientific literacy is exceedingly important because of the interrelationships between science, technology, national security, and economic health. Some businesses, therefore, tend to be surprisingly literate, at least in terms of technology, regardless of how well educated their individual executives themselves may be. The legal profession, however, has little or no reason to be scientifically literate except in cases involving modern forensics or industries that are heavily dependent on technology. But lawyers and businessmen can, and often do, hire their scientific literacy in the form of consultants and expert witnesses, either of which may be quite literate, but neither of which is particularly constrained by the unwritten laws of real science. In other words, consultants and expert witnesses don't necessarily do science; instead, they are skilled *consumers* and *users* of science.

134

Scientific literacy refers to the ability to read scientific information, interpret graphs and figures, understand evidence used to support arguments about scientific and technological issues, and evaluate sources of data used to support public actions. Scientific literacy thus depends on education, but not necessarily what we typically think of as "science education" in the public school sense. Instead, true scientific literacy depends on what we might call "deep" education, that is, the kind that changes the way we view the world. For example, we might claim that having a vague sense of what a molecule is, and perhaps even being able to define the term, counts as being at least somewhat scientifically literate. After all, you have a word and an idea in your mind and you're not completely baffled when you hear the word spoken on television or read it in the newspaper. Furthermore, you might actually be able to use this word in a complete sentence, such as "I wonder whether the molecules in these pills will make me sick if I swallow them with good Irish whiskey," or "I wonder whether some of the molecules in that bag of lawn chemicals will kill my cat." These particular sentences reveal an incipient scientific-type curiosity capable of sustaining a deep education, whereas the sentence "Don't bother me with all that talk about molecules, just give me something to cure this headache" reveals a naïveté typical of the scientifically illiterate.

Deep education is manifested when you incorporate the idea of a molecule into your daily decision making, regardless of whether the decisions are simple easy ones (whether to put sugar or artificial sweetener on your cereal) or more long-term and difficult ones (to stop taking your prescribed medicine because of a newspaper report on associated side effects in a small number of cases). In the first instance, you feel comfortable making the simple decision because you also have a third choice—neither—and you don't know anyone who's actually been hurt by either sugar or artificial sweetener, at least in single doses. Your molecular decision may be influenced by your weight on any particular day, your weight on previous days, your desired weight, or the feeling of having achieved a goal relative to weight control. Although the decision to use sugar or substitute is a pretty trivial one in scientific terms, when that decision becomes part of an overall engagement with matters of diet and weight control, especially for sound and healthy reasons, then the decision indicates a fairly sophisticated engagement with biology as a science, albeit at a highly personal level. And, if you actually read labels on food products and understand most of what they contain, you're well on your way toward becoming scientifically literate.

In the second instance the decision to stop taking a prescription drug is more troublesome because you really don't have much control over many of the factors that contributed to your possession of this supply of molecules. You did not write the prescription; your doctor wrote it based on observations that you might know but probably don't completely understand. You don't have any information beyond what's written in the newspaper about serious side effects or from various web sites, some of them maintained by the pharmaceutical industry and others provided by kooks. In the best of all worlds you quit taking the medicine and don't notice much difference in your health because the medicine wasn't having any dramatic effects anyway (this was actually the case with me and a drug prescribed for joint pain). In the worst of all worlds you start worrying about potential side effects and can't seem to get a straight answer from your doctor or HMO. So it becomes a relief when the company that manufactures this drug pulls it from the market. A deep decision has been made for you, but the fact that this company removed it from the shelves also is a little disturbing, especially if that drug was a profitable one and if, as a result of your curiosity about prescription medications, you're suddenly more curious about the pharmaceutical industry than you might have been before.

Decisions that I've called "deep" are ones that involve both a breadth of scientific knowledge and a propensity, derived from an understanding of science as a way of knowing, to evaluate evidence supporting an assertion and to think in comparative terms. Deep decisions accept the fundamental nature of science: its dependence on observations, the independence of those observations from your desires or beliefs, and the fact that to be relevant, observations must function to test a testable assertion (prediction). Such decisions also accept the idea of probability and the fact of statistical variation instead of demanding certainty. In the case of the sugar substitute decision, you may well have shown a high level of scientific literacy if you engaged in all the label reading and diet design activities intended to keep you healthy and actually knew why you were doing these acts. In addition, such literacy probably primed you to acquire further scientific knowledge and understanding if needed, for example, when faced with a significant environmental issue affecting your property values. But you may also know, and be comfortable with this knowledge, that *usually* and *probably* have legitimate meanings based on statistical analysis. Thus the "chance" that you will have an adverse reaction to a drug is based on observations of populations, and it sort of in the same category as the "chance" that it will rain today, provided both estimates are given to you by doctors and meteorologists respectively.

Back to diet. If you're convinced that dietary awareness, exercise, and label reading keeps your weight and cholesterol under control, then you're sort of a walking experiment but with a sample size of one and no control group with which to compare yourself. Nevertheless, you have a testable assertion regarding your own body and through your activity you are testing that assertion about weight and blood chemistry, and probably also self-esteem. Regardless of the sample size and lack of control group, you are making decisions that affect yourself and perhaps others, such as family members, using knowledge about the natural world, and using that knowledge in a rational way consistent with scientific practice. The alternate version of this assertion, that if you consume large quantities of certain kinds of molecules you will become heavier and less healthy (as revealed by a bathroom scale and the blood work at annual physical exam time), also is well within your power to test, but your decision not to test it is an example of one based on a meaningful relationship between desire and nature. Thus nature will allow you to fulfill your desire, at least to a certain extent, provided you interact with nature in a way suggested by scientific knowledge about how nature—your body—works.

As indicated in the previous chapter, testable assertions are the hallmark of science, but in the political arena, assertions usually are testable only within an historical framework. Politics is an historical discipline with its own rules of evidence that may not match those of science. Within the realm of history, you can't really do "experiments," as we properly define the term; you can only assess the validity of some assertion by looking back on what actually happened when you acted as if that assertion (prediction) were true. An excellent example of such prediction testing is the Iraq war that began with the invasion of that nation by a group of other nations, led mostly by the United States, in 2003. The assertions were that the sovereign nation of Iraq (1) had or was developing, and intended to use, "weapons of mass destruction," (2) would quickly adopt an American-style democracy once their dictator was overthrown, and (3) would be a business-friendly working environment shortly after hostilities ceased. All of these predictions were tested and shown to be false. But unlike a real experiment such as one involving bacterial metabolism, you can't go back and start over with wars of choice, or, for that matter, with wars of necessity.

The vast majority of all politicians rely on public approval to sustain their employment. In addition, once in office, the trappings of power can become quite seductive. These two facets of political life are among the main reasons that politicians are so scientifically illiterate, or at least often act as if they are. Nevertheless, most if not all positions occupied by politicians also involve major responsibilities, compliance with various laws, ceremonial activities, and nowadays, public scrutiny of religious beliefs and behaviors demonstrating "faith." Nobody who professes to be an atheist should be so stupid as to spend money running for public office in the United States of America, no matter how lowly that office might be or how qualified the individual. Elected membership on the Lancaster County, Nebraska, Weed Control Authority comes immediately to mind; no self-proclaimed secular humanists need apply. Thus politicians are scientifically illiterate, or act as if they are, because the demands of public office, the need for public approval, and the constant scrutiny of their faith-based behavior, all job-related phenomena that work to make such literacy a liability instead of an asset. Anyone who believes that conflict between science and religion ended with Galileo is quite naïve.

Besides the factors of responsibility, approval, and scrutiny, it also is important to remember that mobs want answers and solutions from their leaders, not questions and problems. In general, science tends to produce more questions and problems than answers and solutions. This tendency derives from the fundamental nature of science as an activity and probably is best explained by the metaphor of an Island of Understanding in a Sea of Ignorance. Remember that as an island grows in size (increase in understanding), its shoreline (the boundary between understanding and ignorance) also grows. All the questions and problems lie along this boundary. In addition, to continue with the metaphor, the larger an island gets, the more geographically diverse it tends to be; this principle is well illustrated by existing real islands. If that geographic diversity involves mountains, then we have a high perch from which to observe the sea of ignorance. Routinely such observation shows that sea to be much larger than we imagined when we were only down on our hands and knees in the sand studying nature at the [metaphorical] shore.

The familiar case of New Orleans vs. Hurricane Katrina beautifully illustrates all these points about breadth of knowledge, comparative thinking, observations, history, and the basic properties of science. Breadth of knowledge is perhaps the most important factor that should have been considered in the political decisions involving the Mississippi Delta ecology. A broadly educated politician would never simply ask how much money an ecological project—for example, a system of levees and an artificial river (the New Orleans shipping channel)—costs, or how much money the public is willing to spend on such a project. Instead, as a minimum, a broadly educated politician considers history, socio-economic conditions, the probability of disaster, the quality of expertise consulted, whether or not that expertise is in agreement with other expertise from diverse sources, the nature of observations, the process of analysis, and whether the process itself has obvious flaws or internal contradictions. Thus to really assess the adequacy of New Orleans levees, one would have to study the Mississippi Delta using approaches that would be quite familiar to any evolutionary biologist.

Research over the past half century, an activity increasing both the size of our island of understanding and the length of its shoreline boundary with the sea of ignorance, clearly revealed (produced) more questions and problems about the Mississippi Delta region than answers and solutions. Such research involved new technologies such as satellite imagery, geographic information system software, and socio-economic analysis, as well as experience derived from study of the Achafalaya River and its basin using more conventional methods—measurement of stream flow, sedimentation and erosion rates, pressures on diversion dams and gates, etc. Over the years, the scientific community came to realize that the initial problem and its solution, namely, keeping water out of New Orleans by building levees, was actually only a small part of a much larger problem, specifically, long term management of the interrelationship between a nation's economy and one of the world's largest rivers.

This kind of collective activity, in which a truly massive ecosystem is the primary player at the center of a highly integrated, far-reaching, transportation and financial network, does not lend itself to governance by mobs that want answers and solutions instead of questions and problems from their leaders. Instead, this kind of system requires almost Jeffersonian dignity, patience, foresight, and breadth, traits that don't survive well in our Third Millennium media-driven electioneering environment.

Such a broad education, and its use in a public arena, is therefore a lot, indeed probably too much, to ask of any modern politician. But then, of course, it is the job of any television, web site, or newspaper reporter halfway qualified for his or her job to ask the right questions of elected officials in order to reveal their breadth of knowledge, in situations involving natural phenomena, or, in the best of all worlds, to inspire those politicians to acquire knowledge, wisdom, and some decent honest advisers who are not just sycophants. Sadly, perhaps for reasons that are deeply embedded in the human DNA, as a general rule, reporters are hardly more patient than mobs with careful analysis, complex interactions between elements of nature, varying degrees of probability, and leaders who are honest about the chances that disaster will befall us. Instead, we seem to admire leaders who are strong advocates of actions based on our beliefs and desires, who inspire us to be courageous, and who tend to simplify a complex universe down to issues and explanations we can understand. Such leaders make good press. And leaders who can convince us we are in danger, and seem to be fighting that danger in an obvious way, not only are the ones we seem to admire the most, they also make great press. None of this typical interaction between a population and its chosen leaders promotes scientific literacy or honesty about the relationship between nature and our species, *Homo sapiens*.

I do not claim that scientists, because they are scientists, are more honest or broadly educated than politicians. But in the realm of science, the honesty system operates much more strongly and rapidly than in the realm of politics, mainly because this system typically involves anonymous review of scientific work before that work is made public, and it does not involve public decision-making or voting by a diverse electorate. If you are doing experiments on the sex life of some tiny worm and try to publish your results, then an anonymous but well-educated scientist will scrutinize your methods, including your experimental design, your statistical analysis, your rationale for doing the project in the first place, your interpretations of the results, the extent to which you have taken existing knowledge into account, and even the quality of your writing. All this review does not necessarily make you an honest person, but it does tend to pick up flaws in your thinking and mistakes in your actions. But if you go to a cocktail party filled with attorneys and elected city officials, the main question you are likely to be asked about your research is: "Why is this kind of stuff important?" The question really means: "Why are you spending time and money, maybe even tax money, on this kind of activity, and why do you seem to be so interested in sex?"

There may be a thousand good reasons why you are studying the sex life of obscure worms, but these reasons probably involve the fundamental nature of science itself. The worms could, potentially, become a model system for the study of hormone action at the cellular level, thus serving to help explain developmental anomalies in humans, livestock, and companion animals. The worms might be extraordinarily beautiful creatures under the microscope, thus quite attractive to students who in turn could easily become internationally renowned scholars studying an important global human affliction but who remember fondly their carefree undergrad days back in the lab when all they had to talk about was worm sex. The worms' reproductive biology could easily shed light on the origin of sex itself, or the evolution of pheromones, both subjects of enormous interest to the scientific community. Pheromone action, as you might suspect, also could be of substantial interest to the cosmetics industry. When a scientist hears that another scientist is studying the sex life of obscure worms, then all of the possibilities mentioned in this paragraph usually come to mind because scientists typically understand how science itself works on a grand scale. But politicians, like their constituencies, rarely get past the issues of time, money (especially tax money), and sex, although sometimes, if not often, there is a hidden disdain for people who would spend their lives studying microscopic creatures with no immediate economic importance.

In our example of the worms, politicians' focus on time, money, sex, and utility is not necessarily stupid, evil, or dangerous, although it has the potential for being all three. In the previous paragraph, I've actually revealed all the reasons why in order to remain economically competitive in a technologically competitive world, a nation needs to have a strong, healthy, broad, and active scientific enterprise. *Flourishing scientific activity, sustained largely by curiosity about the natural world, breeds scientists, models, new ways of studying nature, and new applications of existing technology.* Thus it is the *human resources* that are of prime importance to a highly developed nation, not the discoveries themselves. Given enough human resources engaged in research, techniques for studying heretofore mysterious aspects of nature will be developed and the discoveries will be made. Furthermore, breadth of research interest tends to produce transferable technologies, a critical factor in sustaining a technology-based economy.

The laser (light amplification by stimulated emission) is perhaps the best example of this phenomenon from twentieth-century science in the United States. A brief history of the laser's technological development can be found on the Bell Labs web site (www.bell-labs.com/history/laser), but in essence, two scientists—Arthur L. Schawlow and Charles H. Townes—developed the technology from research that began in the 1940s. Schawlow was a researcher at Bell Labs, and Townes was a consultant to the Bell Labs research enterprise. These scientists' primary interest at the time was molecular structure, and the laser was intended to be a device to help them pursue their research. The commercial development of laser technology, along with its rapid spread throughout almost all aspects of modern American life, can be traced to the publication of a paper entitled *Infrared and Optical Masers* (in *Physical Review*, volume 112, pages 1940–1949, published December 15, 1958). You can read this original piece of science simply by doing a Google search using the title—*Infrared and Optical Masers*—as your search term. Now we have laser pointers in the classroom, laser surgery in the hospital, laser scanning in the grocery story, etc. Although the laser may be the most easily understood example of transferable technology, our daily lives are filled with other cases. And, of course, science feeds on itself in this regard, with practicing scientists always trying creative applications for new and existing technologies.

Another history lesson—actually a rule of human resource development—that politicians typically fail to understand is the following: *Artists often spring quickly, even spontaneously, out of a population, but scientists do not.* Technological advances and economically important innovations might periodically emerge out of the realm of basic science, but the "realm of basic science" requires a vastly different cultural milieu than does the intellectual soup that spawns artists, poets, writers, and musicians. Any nation that does not outright suppress or punish artists will end up with a good supply of them, especially if there is some obvious duplicity or incompetence in high places to generate cynicism. But to be economically competitive in the Third Millennium, nations need lots of healthy, authentic, curiosity-driven, scientists and such individuals are not guaranteed to arise, and become legitimate scientists, by virtue of their own two hands and a paintbrush (two hands and a guitar, a pencil and a bar napkin, etc.). Science needs physical facilities, computational power, technology, ready access to information on a global scale, time, patience, and lots of people. To be economically competitive in the Third Millennium, a nation does not need a bunch of ignorant elected officials, afraid of science, afraid of the word *evolution*, and afraid of anything that seems to support immoral behavior. A nation needs, instead, a bunch of courageous, well-educated, and intellectually honest human beings who have the interpersonal and verbal skills to help inform citizens on scientific matters, and especially on the link between economic health and a valid understanding of how nature operates.

Scientifically literate citizens understand, or at least appreciate, the variability inherent in study design, sometimes dubious reliability of data on social issues, and the ideology built into assertions by politicians. Scientifically literate citizens always ask first about evidence that a particular assertion will be, or has been, true. One excellent example of an assertion that probably should have been subject to close scrutiny typically reserved for peer reviews of scientific studies was Public Law 107-110, otherwise known as the 2001 No Child Left Behind Act (NCLB). The assertion (= testable hypothesis) was this one: "A combination of standardized testing and threatened punishment for low performance on such tests will significantly improve the levels of math and science literacy among American school children, especially the most disadvantaged ones." Any teacher knows that this testable hypothesis is actually a formula for derailing an educational system that might be doing about as well as could be expected, given the resources, parental involvement, and economic status of students' families. Thus if you're threatened with punishment because of low standardized test scores, you teach to the test. If you're required by law to report performance by student category, then you divert human resources into reporting. As any scientist could have predicted, the main result of NCLB legislation was a booming statistics industry and a generation of teachers and students who are far more concerned with the answer to a particular question than with acquisition of transferable skills.

Is scientific literacy important to a modern society? Yes. Literacy in general, not just scientific, is of profound importance to any civilized society, or, for that matter, to any civilization that is to sustain itself in a particular environment. Of course *literacy* can refer to any domain of information, so that in truly primeval societies such as African Pygmies or the western New Guinea highlands Ndani, the ability to read and interpret signs in the forest is just as important as an ability to read street signs or graffiti marking gang territory boundaries would be to an urban American. But scientific literacy is a special kind of literacy because scientific discoveries can spread quickly throughout the human population, producing massive changes in economics, political power, and the relationships between nations. Nuclear technology is the best modern example of this phenomenon.

Science literacy also addresses our long-term and widespread relationships with the planet. Fossil fuel production, climate change, and tropical deforestation are examples of science- and technology-dependent phenomena that fall into this category. These relationships with nature are crucial ones because Earth is the only planet known to support human life, and we are humans. Now, having said that, I admit that vast numbers of people believe that this planet is doomed to obliteration, that Earth is only a temporary home for our bodies, that our spirits will live for Eternity in some far-off place, and so whatever actions we take here and now are not really very important in the long term. A study of history suggests, and fairly strongly, that such thinking makes truly bad foreign and economic policy.

Widespread scientific literacy is crucial to the welfare of any so-called developed nation for several reasons. First, most such nations are heavily armed, and in the Third Millennium, armaments are fairly sophisticated machines built using technology derived from our understanding of substances and forces present throughout the universe and in accordance with various scientific principles. We can believe in Heaven but faith alone cannot direct a missile to its correct target; instead, we need computers, software, sensors, explosives, propellant mixtures, transportation, electronic communications, and highly trained people, all products of a scientific enterprise. If we are at war, science allows us to aim our weapons at the enemy instead of at ourselves. And if we view war, and the potential for war, as a major economic engine, as we obviously do in the United States, then basic science to support technological development is crucial to a large segment of our economy.

Second, scientific literacy is vital to a developed nation because so many of our public policies, especially ones having economic impacts, are linked to management of natural phenomena. Good examples of this relationship include water allocation, crop subsidies, energy resource development and utilization, natural disaster preparedness, the provision of health care, flood plain designations, and zoning. There may be public debate over "environmental issues," but in the end Mother Nature will decide how much rain to deliver and when to deliver it, how much corn can be produced on an acre of Iowa farm land, and whether to bash New Orleans into oblivion or break San Francisco off the country and dump it into the Pacific Ocean. So "debate over environmental issues" really translates into a contest between what we know and understand about the way nature works and what we want to have happen. Scientific literacy shapes this contest between reality and desire.

The ongoing fight between reality and desire is perhaps the most important reason of all for a nation's citizens to be, on the average, scientifically literate. Scientists have a certain mindset, one that is governed by evidence, observation, and technology, and in which interpretations or conclusions are always subject to modification based on additional information. In the vast majority of cases, this scientist's approach to his or her profession carries over into everyday life outside the laboratory. Scientists certainly are not alone in exhibiting this particular type of behavior; artists, attorneys, and physicians, indeed virtually all of us, tend to view the world through lenses shaped by our professions. But we need to remember the fundamental nature of science: an exploration of the universe using falsifiable assertions as the primary working tool, assertions that are developed within the context of a general explanatory theory. This character of science explains why scientists tend to believe that in the long run, reality forced upon us by planetary processes will override desire if the two are in conflict.

Because of its defining character, the scientific enterprise generates some rules about evidence used to support assertions about reality and the practicality of desires. Scientists typically heap scorn on untestable assertions, good examples of which can be found daily in American political discourse and indeed throughout American domestic policy of the Third Millennium. Scientists are equally scornful of assertions for which the supporting evidence is exceedingly flimsy, borderline unattainable, or subject to severe sampling flaws. Some of these assertions are so burdened with ideological baggage that studies to test them, while technically possible, are not always politically possible. Again, our public political discourse provides ample illustrations of such assertions. Here are a few familiar ones:

(1) Abstinence-only sex education in public schools will significantly reduce sexual activity among teenage children, unwanted pregnancy, the incidence of sexually transmitted disease, and abortion.

(2) A combination of standardized testing and threatened punishment for low performance on such tests will significantly improve the levels of math and science

literacy among American school children, especially the most disadvantaged ones.

(3) Reducing taxes for the wealthier Americans will improve the economic status of all Americans.

(4) Some kind of a national health care program will bring economic ruin to the United States.

(5) Prescription drugs purchased in Canada are a public health hazard.

(6) Elimination of prayer in public schools leads to moral decay of the nation.

(7) Hollywood is eroding American moral fiber with its never-ending supply of sex and violence.

This list could be longer, and with a little bit of effort, any American could add to it just by reading the newspaper or listening to the radio. Thus we are besieged with assertions that seem to be congruent with our internal logic ("If we 'teach' abstinence then teens will be abstinent.") yet to the scientific mind fail for all the above-mentioned reasons. Inadequacy of data, which reflects mostly an inability to actually obtain relevant data, probably tops the list of these reasons. Assertions which cannot be tested because we can't actually design the studies and get the appropriate numbers are highly effective political weapons, but these weapons tend to be used on members of the society that develops them instead of on enemies, perceived or real. We turn our arguments upon ourselves and the fact that they cannot be scientifically evaluated means they never go away.

As an example of an untestable assertion, consider the first one on the above list: abstinence education. We would need several experimental groups (carefully matched economically, ethnically, and demographically), and several control groups (not taught anything about sex), just to start a truly legitimate scientific study. Modern studies involving humans all require approval by oversight committees, usually ones associated with medical schools, and such approval involves informed consent waivers, which in turn require either adult status or parental signatures. Imagine some scientist coming into a PTA meeting to inform assembled parents of middle school children of this study and its design. You now have an

explanation why this assertion about the effects of abstinence education is essentially untestable. After-the-fact surveys can provide a sort of test, and in this particular case the
assertion (= hypothesis) is generally conceded to be rejected.
Readily available information indicates that abstinence-only
sex education classes don't have any observable long-term
effect on teenage pregnancy rates (see Internet source in the
"Acknowledgments, Notes, and Sources" chapter). Any good
biologist could have predicted this outcome, although probably with a touch of sarcasm derived from knowledge of wild-
animal breeding behavior.

Survey data usually are at least somewhat indicative of
attitudes and resulting social change, but tend to be highly
variable in quality. Such data are subject to bias arising from
ignorance, improperly phrased questions, inadequate sampling strategies, and population traits hidden from people
conducting the survey. These potential failings support a professional polling industry, the Gallup International organiza-
tion being a prime example. Survey design professionals try to
write questions that are self-validating, reveal specific attrib-
utes, and minimize emotional impact. If you are contacted by
someone being paid to collect survey data, and if you are willing to answer the questions, you may be asked as many as
twenty, and sometimes up to fifty, questions about how likely
you are to exhibit some kind of behavior, with responses limited to phrases such as "very likely," "somewhat likely," "somewhat unlikely," and "not likely." The behavior can range from
voting for a certain candidate to buying a certain service or
product. Among the questions will be some internal validating
ones which you may not recognize as such. Thus if you
answer a particular question with "very likely," you will probably also answer the validation question the same way,
assuming you are telling the pollster the truth about your
experiences, attitudes, or behaviors.

Surveys give us information, but are they science? This
question is one that scientists themselves argue about, often
choosing an answer based on academic politics. A survey of
insects that live in a particular location, a survey of plant
species on a prairie, a survey of parasite species that occur in

some hosts—are these lists the product of science? Are the people who develop these lists real scientists? After all, the data provide a test of a testable assertion: so-and-so lives here. Furthermore, the research can produce tangible evidence, such as museum specimens and DNA, for what the universe is like at a particular time and place. Such surveys routinely stimulate further investigation, giving rise to "why" questions while enlarging the perimeter of our Island of Understanding. And over time, if repeated, they can tell us what's happening to our planet as a result of human activities. So yes, surveys— the systematic gatherings of information—can be considered science, and public policy stemming from survey results can be considered technology.

Is there reason for optimism among scientists in this Great American Experiment run mostly by politicians and business men and women? That is a good question, probably with as many answers as there are people calling themselves scientists and residing within our borders. If there is a reason to be optimistic, then it rests on the nature of our political dialog. If this dialog is characterized by prediction ("Doing _____ will raise taxes and increase crime.") then there is little reason for optimism. If the dialog is characterized mainly by problems and relevant statistics ("Your tax increase is the equivalent of one twenty-ounce pop a month and closing the library on Sundays will have the greatest negative impact on lower-income users.") then there is reason for everyone, not just scientists, to be optimistic because such conversation demonstrates that someone has learned from past experience.

8 WHY ARE POLITICIANS SO SCIENTIFICALLY ILLITERATE?

"...go live where our minds take us...;"

What is a Human Being?

A theory that explains eating by man's digestive system cannot explain also why different societies obtain and prepare food in different ways, or why some have food taboos and others do not.

—Peter Farb, *Man's Rise to Civilization*

This question—*What is a human being?*—is the leading question of our time and it can be answered in about seven billion ways, that is, in as many ways as there are people on Earth. At two of many extremes are answers leading to the so-called creation-evolution controversy: (1) A human being is a special creation made by God in His image; or (2) A human being is a highly evolved ape, a species whose biology is dictated by bipedalism, an opposable thumb, and a hypertrophied cerebral cortex. There is little to be gained by denying that humans are animals, specifically mammals, whose physiology and genetics are in most ways very similar to those of other mammals, especially pigs and great apes (chimpanzees, gorillas, and orangutans). Anyone who denies this similarity reveals a deep and inexcusable ignorance about life on Earth, or else a political agenda in which ignorance is a weapon. The genetic and physiological similarity between people and other animal species is undeniable; it is an observed fact. Medical research, with all its discoveries and health-related technology, rests firmly on this similarity.

But humans are not exactly identical to other species, either genetically or physiologically, and certainly not mentally. The genetic and physiological differences are well known and taken into account during trials of new medical procedures. Our brains, however, set us an almost indescribable distance apart from other species, not so much in terms of neuron function or motor responses to stimuli, but in terms of that emergent property we call the "mind." Thus we have the capacity to create worlds, indeed whole universes, out of only thoughts, ideas, words, and pictures. We have no idea whether other species can perform this remarkable feat, and we really don't have the tools—intellectual or otherwise—to even conduct the studies necessary to determine whether orangutans can make fantasy worlds where they go hang out when life in the trees gets boring or stressful. But if we have a single defining trait, it is our ability to make something out of nothing, then go live where our minds have taken us, devoting considerable time, energy, and money to such imaginary travel, and in the process acting as if our constructions are truly natural phenomena.

This trait—that of being able to build a fantasy house then live in it—is of short-time economic value only under certain environmental conditions. Those conditions require that we be free of the responsibility for finding food, water, and shelter in the wilderness, and for avoiding real predators. Civilization generates just such freedom, at least for large numbers of us. The mind's most wonderful and outrageous creations therefore can be considered products of socio-economic systems characterized by exploitation of natural resources, division of labor, and especially production of leisure time.

Lest we equate such systems with post-WWII northern hemisphere developed nations, we must remember that for centuries, human beings, including those in so-called primitive societies, have produced absolutely wondrous art, literature, and music, along with highly effective technology designed specifically for the natural environments occupied by those societies. The more "primitive" literature may be relatively inaccessible except to those already educated in appropriate languages and history, and the music may grate on our rap-trained ears, but the art is on display around the world, most dramatically, perhaps, in the Musée du Quai Branly in Paris. This relatively new and striking $333-million architectural statement houses thousands of pieces of non-Western art, and the collection, preservation, and display of such anthropologically significant material is the museum's primary mission.

Not everyone agrees that the artifacts in Musée du Quai Branly are "art." The pieces are beautiful, visually imposing, and send subliminal messages to a viewer, but unlike, for example, American Abstract Expressionist paintings, such constructions come laden with culture-specific baggage and their designs are deeply intertwined with tribal traditions, oral history, and mythology. Wandering the Branly galleries, a single question surfaces repeatedly: what was going through their *minds* when they made that … [fill in your own item: mask, shawl, stool, etc.]? Yes, indeed, what was going through the *minds* of people making tangible objects, in a particular way, at any place on Earth and in any historical period for what must have been a reason that went well beyond utility but was intimately tied to that utility?

Thus we have one significant answer to this leading question of our time. A human being is an animal for which utility is a necessary feature of constructions, but quickly becomes a secondary property. Our technology is *necessary but not sufficient*, so is only a starting place upon which elaborations are displayed, elaborations that reveal the maker as human. A chimpanzee might strip leaves off a twig to make a tool for extracting termites from a mound, but the chimp does not spend time decorating this twig. A human, on the other hand, carves designs, perhaps of importance in terms of oral history, on a knife handle, then on the shoulder blade of some bison that previously was dinner. A chimpanzee may pick up a limb and use it to bash a competitor, but the animal doesn't save that particular limb, then scratch intricate patterns upon it. Unlike the chimp, a human engraves memorable scenes on weapons, in the process turning them into collectibles. Few would argue that guns are, for example, in and of themselves, art; equally few would deny that the diversity of weaponry available to any law abiding American citizen goes far, indeed, exceedingly far, beyond that required to kill squirrels, ducks, quail, deer, or other people. The weapon is deemed necessary; engraving and diversity make it sufficient.

A human being therefore is an animal that not only produces art, music, and literature, none of which is of immediate utilitarian value, but also turns strictly utilitarian items

154

into a personalized form of art that itself diversifies, almost as if having been invented, so is then free to manifest a phylogeny. For example, we can legitimately speak about the *evolution* of design: of cell phones, automobiles, and thousands, if not tens of thousands, of other artifacts. Furthermore, the reverse also is true, and seemingly useless items always have the potential for transformation into something of lasting economic value. A Rossini overture can, if you stretch your definition of utility a little bit, serve to keep orchestra musicians, stagehands, instrument makers and repairmen, and printers employed, at least at minimal wages, so spread over time, the use of such music is roughly equivalent to the use of some invention—people do things with it, and go to some effort to keep it within the realm of accessible social constructs, and there is money to be made from this work. When there is money to be earned, then bills can be paid and children educated.

Similarly, in utilitarian terms, a Rothko painting is absolutely worthless; nobody ever killed an enemy, fixed a leaky faucet, or took the kids to soccer practice with a Rothko. But museums holding these gloomy abstractions attract thousands of visitors, most of whom pay admission, so money changes hands because someone wants to see a painting made by someone else. People work in security, preservation, the coffee and gift shops, development and fundraising, and education; gift shop items often are crafted by artisans in distant lands and imported from halfway around the world; airline companies, hotels, and taxi drivers all partake of the Rothko mystique indirectly. This flow of money, manufactured goods, and jobs surrounding the visual arts exists because of Rothko and the thousands of others who produced art to satisfy some inner message emanating from their *minds*. An afternoon in London's Tate Modern museum demonstrates clearly the economic value of individual thoughts, visions, and creative acts, with Mark Rothko as the prime example.

The same claim can be made about our fascination with history and the natural world. Globally, various museums preserve our evidence for what the world was and is really like, what we as a species have built, used, and admired. Chimpanzees do not build museums; only humans purposefully resurrect then consume cultures, reflect on the results of our behavior over millennia, and build astronomical observatories. Chichen Itza and Machu Picchu are products of the human mind, especially that part of the mind that wonders about our relationship to the natural world and seeks to define humanity's place in it. The American Museum of Natural History, the Smithsonian Institution, and the Muséum National d'Histoire Naturelle, all are illustrations of our humanity, as much a revelation of our minds at work as the Tate Modern in London and the Museum of Modern Art in New York City.

The list of museums in Paris alone is pages long, and although Paris is probably the finest example of humanity's preoccupation with itself and the place it lives, all major cities have an impressive number of similar institutions and the collection/reflection habit extends even to small towns out in the American heartland. Pick out any place in Kansas and do a Google search; chances are excellent you'll find a chamber of commerce tab on the town's web site, and along with it, a list of historical and artistic attractions. Try the Museum of the Fur Trade in Chadron, Nebraska, or the Roller Skating Museum and the Museum of Germans from Russia in that state's capital city, Lincoln. Oklahoma City is awash in such blatant displays of our humanness: The National Cowboy Hall of Fame and Western Heritage Museum, the National Softball Hall of Fame, and the 45th Infantry Division Museum, to name but three of a dozen.

Insofar as we know, chimpanzees don't do genealogies, either, buying software to assist in the exploration of one's own identify, spending hours at the computer tracking down relatives, sending cheek swabs to commercial DNA analysis labs, taking trips back to the homeland, and loading up the mini-van for a long haul to Salt Lake City to search through Mormon Church records. Orangutans don't collect their maternal grandmother's china, their paternal grandmother's silver, or display pictures of their infants in a treetop office.

Gorillas don't put correspondence in museum archives, build Presidential libraries, or write biographies. Non-human animals stare at themselves in mirrors, and we have some evidence that they are aware of their own identity, especially in the case of great apes and elephants, but none of these species has the borderline pathological curiosity about themselves displayed by humans, at least insofar as we know or can determine by existing research methods.

The museums and amateur genealogists of unremarkable communities such as Lincoln, Nebraska, and Oklahoma City, Oklahoma, are not particularly unusual; indeed, they are outright pedestrian examples of our narcissism, a fact that reveals the extent of it. We want to know about ourselves, we want to be reminded of what we have done and where we have been, both literally and figuratively, we want others to know about us, and once we're old enough to master a keyboard, we swarm to MySpace.com and Facebook.com and start broadcasting messages about who we are and who we want to be. Unfortunately, this intense curiosity about other members of our species, including those quite unlike ourselves, is matched by an equally intense repulsion of other humans, especially those who appear on the surface to be quite different from us. The Musée du Quai Branly is predicated on the former; racism, ancient ethnic hatreds, and the Iraq civil war of 2005–? are sustained by the latter. A leading question for theorists in the area of social and developmental psychology might be: how are these two powerful urges—curiosity and repulsion—related? A corollary question could easily be: how do societies make the transition from one to another, or at least reconcile the conflict in a way that does not wreak havoc?

These questions are not merely mental games for academics. As *Homo sapiens* spreads its destructive power across the globe, consuming tropical forests at the rate of fifty acres a minute, stripping the oceans of life (over two million tons of fish and other seafood a year eaten in the U.S.A. alone), sucking its rivers and fossil water supplies dry, burning fossil sunlight like there was an infinite supply (which there is not, and everyone knows it), and killing one another by the tens of thousands a year, the bases for our conflicts and group behaviors should be of truly global concern. In an utopian world, we come to understand why we destroy, fight, kill, and act against our own species' interests, then apply that understanding to resolve conflicts and limit our impact on the planet. But we do not live in utopia, and all efforts to construct one on Earth have been ultimate failures. In response to the leading question of our time—*What is a human being?*—our best answer so far is: a primate that is probably too smart, or at least too self-conscious, for its own good. And even those traits would not spell our downfall were it not for that damned opposable thumb.

The elegance and sophistication of art, music, and literature produced by our species defy description, and their manifestations, made possible largely by available technology, surround us daily. As a handy example, video games are, to some, a symbol of youthful degeneracy, if not an outright dangerous cultural weapon that "Hollywood" has placed in the hands of our innocent children. Nothing could be further from the truth. First, video games generally are designed and produced in places far from Hollywood, although the use of that name as a synonym for "the entertainment industry" is reasonably close to being justified. Second, they are a highly visible demonstration that science and technology typically have multiple applications, and artists have never been reluctant to use technology in ways its developers never intended or imagined.

Third, video games represent exploitation of science and technology for commercial purposes, hardly a behavior foreign to Americans or, for that matter, to modern humans in general. In this country we have an expectation that technology will have commercial applications, and most large American universities have a "technology transfer" office whose *responsibility* it is to make money and political hay off of faculty ideas and research. Finally, these games are little more than stories in which players can become involved as participants; in this last sense, they can be classified in the same general category as whatever tales were told around

Cro-Magnon fires by a shaman/artist crawling out of the hole where he'd been painting a wooly mammoth a quarter-mile deep in some secret and sacred chamber.

A human being is, in the final analysis, an ape that tells stories, only a fraction of which are true, then acts on the lessons of those stories regardless of their veracity. This habit, and the capacity, are intimately linked to our fantasy worlds, the ones we create then go live in, whether those worlds be the ones of novelists, wannabe professional football team owners, or even elected public officials declaring that some faraway peoples who have never in their wildest dreams ever wished to vote for a city council member will quickly adopt a representative form of government once our bombs stop falling on them. Furthermore, we see stories in art forms that are not necessarily intended to be narratives, and when those art forms don't have obvious narratives, then we are perfectly capable of finding or creating "backstories."

In fact, the development of *backstory*—a story that explains or justifies another story—is now an accepted, if not expected, element of our literature regardless of the genre or media. The Rothko paintings in London's Tate Modern museum, for example, which in and of themselves "say" little beyond some communication consisting of combination of visual, emotional, and contextual emanations, end up saying plenty when provided with backstory. See Wikipedia to start with a discussion of influences from mythology and Nietzsche, Rothko's travels, and the Rothko Chapel in Houston. The Internet has made Mark Rothko into a readily accessible narrative regardless of, or perhaps in addition to, whatever else he may be. Rothko was simply a handy example; there are at least seven billion others who would serve similarly, although not necessarily as well.

We have absolutely no evidence whatsoever that non-human species use metaphors and other kinds of symbolism in their communications. These literary devices are simply tools to enrich stories and extend their lessons well beyond the literal narrative; Genesis I is a perfect example. Although we have no evidence that chimps or other non-human creatures use metaphors, there is a lot of evidence that they use *paralanguage*, defined as word-equivalents uttered in particular manners and in various contexts, perhaps combined with posture and facial expression, and thus communicating something quite different from the literal translation. Paralanguage may be the primary form of visual/oral communication between non-human vertebrates and among many invertebrate species as well.

As an illustration of this phenomenon of paralanguage, consider the simple phrase "Happy Birthday to you." Most of us in the United States have said this phrase and sung it many times. We've heard it at our own birthdays, and at restaurants sung in obnoxious clapping ways by the wait staff. Within my own family, the song has evolved into an excuse to communicate with our children in a special way, typically early in the morning before any of them really wants to be awake. My wife's birthday is in August, and since childhood it has always been a special day for her, so I ignore it at my peril. My birthday is in late December, thus quite subordinate to Christmas, which my parents celebrated mainly because they probably felt like they had to instead of wanted to, and so I don't remember my birthday ever being important to anyone, especially me, and it still isn't. I cannot remember a single instance in which someone or some group has sung "Happy Birthday" to me. Even if Marilyn Monroe had sung it to me, especially in the way she sang it to John F. Kennedy, I would not have heard any of the words.

"Happy Birthday to you," for example, means many things to many people, only one of which is really "Happy Birthday." The same could be said of "I love you," "go to Hell," and probably every other phrase uttered by a human being. Thus as is the case with other of our traits, we do the same things that non-human mammals, and often birds, do, but we do those things in a much richer, more complex, manner, and we use the traits in ways perhaps uniquely human. Our paralanguage comes to include our economic condition, the cars we drive, the bumper stickers on those cars, our clothing, the furniture in our homes, the subjects of our conversations, the magazines we read, cell phone ring tones we download, desktop wallpaper on our laptops ... this list could easily go on for several pages. Words are the essential vehicle for our communication, but human words really are only the equivalent of a stage; paralanguage is the play.

Language and paralanguage are, of course, inextricably linked to behavior, both that of individuals and that of mobs. And of all our defining traits, there is one expressed in behavior that perhaps characterizes us best of all, serving as a summary of all others. Like most of our other seemingly defining traits, this one also is found among non-human species, but is never manifested to the same extent, at the species level, as ours. And what is this so-called behavioral "trait"? It is the difference between our behavior as individuals and our behavior as a group, so can probably be considered meta-behavior. Virtually all of our highest achievements, from science, mathematics, and engineering, to art, music, and literature, are mainly the work of individuals, although admittedly sometimes those individuals led groups of varying size. Virtually all of our most regrettable and despicable acts, throughout all recorded history, are the work of societies, or at least of large, well-organized groups. If anyone needs a clear demonstration that language and paralanguage can make large groups behave in self-destructive ways, he or she need only study the George W. Bush and Dick Cheney speeches that dragged the United States into that economic black hole known as the second Gulf, or Iraq, War.

The human tragedy, of course, is that these mob actions are so often initiated, and subsequently driven, by individuals in positions of power, those exhibiting "leadership." If our species has a fundamental design flaw it is this willingness to let individuals lead groups astray. The most irreverent among us extends that line of thought to organized religion. The most patient and reflective scientists consider such self-destructive group behavior, inspired by individuals that somehow bubble up into positions of extreme influence, to be little more than an inherited trait suddenly become dangerous in a highly technological world built by the very species that possesses such fossil behavior, a behavior more appropriate for survival of roving *Australopithecus* bands than for modern developed nations dragged into a global economy.

All of the above discussion defines us by what we do, assuming that our identity as individuals, as states and nations, and as a species, lies in our deeds. Scientists, especially biologists, are not bound by such assumptions. Lewis Thomas, for example, in his surprising bestseller book *Lives of a Cell: Notes of a Biology Watcher* (1974), summarized our knowledge of evolutionary biochemistry by pointing out that he personally, and by implication all of us, are products of an ancient invasion in which bacteria, or their ancestors, colonized other cells, then devolved into mitochondria, the structures that convert simple sugars to useable energy for all familiar plants and animals. Thomas was relieved not to have to take responsibility for controlling mitochondrial chemical reactions in order to read the newspaper. He ended up defining our species as a community of microorganisms.

Richard Dawkins followed Thomas' literary achievement with a now classic work in biology: *The Selfish Gene* (1976), which reduced all Earth's inhabitants to mere carriers of nucleotide sequences, the real players in the epic saga of life on a lonely planet. Dawkins' view is that evolution is best depicted as a contest between blocks of genetic information, and that in the larger scheme of things our bodies, as well as those of all past and present organisms, are simply vehicles by which these genes compete with one another for opportunities to persist and multiply. But Dawkins came full circle with his analysis, perhaps inadvertently, by coining the word *meme*, which refers to ideas, innovations, even phrases, that move through human populations in a manner strongly analogous to mutant alleles. In Dawkins' final analysis we can be defined as *human* by our ideas, inventions, and language regardless of how selfishly those entities behave, proliferate, come to dominate their realms, or go extinct. A case, maybe even a very strong case, probably could be made for the assertion that our stories rule us.

Virologists, however, equipped with almost surrealistic molecular technology, tell even a more intriguing, and even startling, story about our genetic makeup: much of the human genome consists of viral sequences, molecular memories, one might say, of ancient and repeated colonization. This discovery is not entirely unexpected, given that science has known for a long time that many if not most organisms contain DNA sequences revealing ancient symbioses, and that genes themselves can and do experience duplication, with gene progeny then moving to different chromosomes, giving rise to offspring of their own, and living an evolutionary life that may or may not coincide with that of their vehicles—the larger and more familiar organisms that carry these genes around to work and play. Alien scientists, visiting us with the analytical tools of modern molecular biologists, could easily conclude that Earth was a planet of microbes, some of which had the misfortune to end up in an environment that seemed determined to make itself extinct—us.

◆   ◆   ◆

Obviously this initial question—What is a human being?—is one that can be answered honestly in only one way: we are what the scientists tell us we are, but that scientific answer reveals a rather wondrous mammal whose deeds, both good and bad, continually exceed our expectations. Has our initial question always been the leading one regardless of when and where it was being asked? Probably; based on our limited knowledge of history, especially that of diverse cultures, many of which are now extinct, we might honestly conclude that all the stories, rituals, practices, traditions, and arts of those cultures were focused on defining humanity for a particular group in a particular time, place, and ecological setting. And throughout history, again insofar as our knowledge lets us see into distant realms, the dehumanization that so often is a prelude to violence also is predicated upon differences in beliefs, practices, traditions, rituals, and stories.

Thus it is a small wonder that people kill one another so readily over differences in religion; indeed, such behavior, so deeply embedded in our species' genetic makeup, is to be expected, and methods to counter this behavior should be the primary focus of whatever training we provide to potential diplomats. When our founding fathers tried to separate religion—that most powerful means of both awarding and withholding membership in our species—from the state—that most powerful means of conducting sanctioned violence—they recognized just how pervasive and all-consuming is our attempt to answer the leading question of our time and place—*What is a human being?*—or our willingness to use the answer for both good and evil, no matter what the calendar date, the latitude, or the longitude.

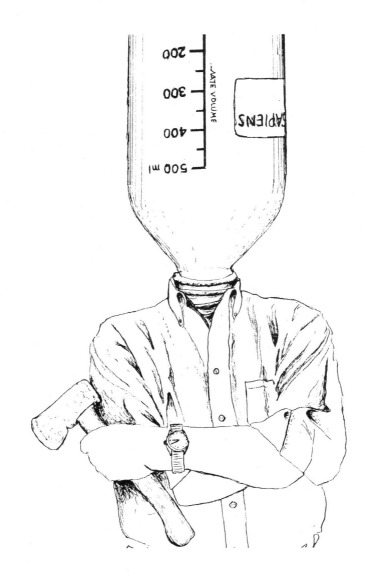

What Will Human Life Be Like in a Couple of Thousand Years?

In all likelihood, any civilization that we can detect will be more advanced than our own, providing us with a glimpse of what Earth's future could be. For the first time, we will witness the history of the future, not just of the past.

> —Frank Drake and Dava Sobel,
> *Is Anyone Out There?*

Obviously there is no way to answer this question of the title for certain, but we can do a little thought experiment that might suggest some answers. Picture yourself in what is now Israel at the time of Jesus' crucifixion attempting to predict what human life would be like in the year 2010 and you will have a sense of the difficulty in making such predictions. On the other hand, what could you have said back then that might be applicable to the problem? The answer is fairly easy: people develop technology (build pyramids, embalm their dead, make catapults and other war machines); practice various religions that are not always compatible; go to war; discriminate against all kinds of people just like we do today (gays, lepers, Philistines, etc.); use their religion to justify behavioral dictums, including highly personal ones involving sex and diet; practice whatever forms of agriculture are allowed by their environments; gather food from the ocean; use narcotics; write, paint, and create art; form pair bonds and produce offspring; and, engage in all sorts of political machinations. People really have not changed much in the past two thousand years except in terms of their available technology, and we don't have much evidence that people differ very much across geographical regions except in terms of cultural traits (learned), at least some of which are adaptations to environment.

Pick any two humans at random from around the world, and if they are of opposite genders, then they can very likely produce viable offspring, assuming they are both of reproductive age and have not been sterilized. Pick any two humans at random from around the world, and if they are both males but of opposite religious beliefs and skin color, there is an excellent chance they might well try to kill one another. These last two sentences could have come from a Bible lesson or the mouth of any modern American who just finished reading the morning newspaper. We are all one species; we have been all one species for at least 50,000 years; but we often act as if we were not all the same species, at least not all *human beings*, in possession of morals, respect, and reason. This disconnect between our biology and our ideals is not likely to be repaired any time soon, particularly not in so short a time as two millennia.

In evolutionary terms, two thousand years is but a hardly measurable blink, so the answer to our question is fairly simple: people two millennia from now will do exactly the same general kinds of things that people do today, except like people of today, or of Jesus' day, they will be limited by their traditions, technology, and environment. Therefore, the answer depends not so much on behavior of people themselves as on cultural traits, technological development, and environmental conditions. Scientists and historians have given us plenty of information to use in making predictions about the general state of technological development and the environmental conditions we can expect two thousand years from now. Indeed, plenty of people have used this information and made predictions ranging from utopian to disastrous. Regardless of specific predictions by various experts, many of whom have personal or political agendas, the historical record is fairly clear. That record tells us two things: (1) you cannot predict technological innovations and developments very accurately or very far in advance, and (2) deteriorating environmental conditions are probably the most important factor in the collapse of civilizations.

Will parts of Earth experience deteriorating environmental conditions severe enough to cause the collapse of various societies and consequently their civil order? The answer is "probably," not so much because I know something nobody else knows, but because the evidence is so strong that such collapses, based on environmental conditions, have happened so frequently in the past. Jared Diamond's compelling book *Collapse: How Societies Choose to Fail or Succeed* provides an easily accessible and beautifully written analysis of this relationship between society and environment and suggests that the process will be repeated again and again in the future. Diamond claims that societies fail when their economies become unsustainable for a variety of reasons, mostly environmental. There is little evidence that Diamond is wrong and plenty that he is correct. So for the purposes of our thought experiment, let's assume he is correct.

Of course any prediction based on this assumption rests firmly on another one, namely, that there will be people on Earth in two thousand years. Two factors could invalidate this second assumption, so we probably need to deal with those factors right up front. In two thousand years, humanity easily could be extinct. We could destroy ourselves with nuclear weapons and make Earth uninhabitable, or a large asteroid could hit our planet somewhere and simply obliterate us, or at least obliterate the resources we need to survive. Invaders from outer space could arrive tomorrow and kill us all. Jesus could return to Earth tomorrow and Rapture could occur about the same time (give or take a week, depending on the particular version of Rapture), all believers could be immediately taken to Heaven, and the rest of the planet denuded. According to the Book of Revelation, there are a couple of thousand-year periods involved in the demise of Earth, so if these prophecies are correct, then humanity as we know it will be rendered extinct by God's hand.

Thought experiments that invoke supernatural forces are not valid ones regardless of how real the gods might be in the minds of believers, how they might in fact seem to behave, or what we believe about their intentions and behaviors. Indeed, the historical record is exceedingly clear in this regard: people will give the gods credit for any natural phenomenon about which they are completely ignorant. The historical record also shows that when we learn how nature operates, suddenly the gods disappear as causal agents although they can easily remain as political forces that inspire human behavior. But in general, people today do what people have done for all recorded history.

For this last reason, I will assume that in two thousand years, there will still be people on Earth developing technology, practicing various religions that are not always compatible, going to war, discriminating against one another, using their religion to justify behavioral dictums, including highly personal ones involving sex and diet, engaging in whatever forms of agriculture are allowed by their environments, gathering food from the ocean, using narcotics, writing, painting, and creating art, forming pair bonds and producing offspring, and engaging in all sorts of political machinations. The question of course is whether in doing all these activities they will resemble the Flintstones more than the Jetsons. Most reasonable scientists would say yes, in two thousand years humans will be living more like the Flintstones than like George Jetson and his family (see "Acknowledgments, Notes, and Sources" if you've forgotten your Saturday morning cartoons from the 1960s).

The main reason for this scientific judgment is the absence of fossil fuels, which surely will disappear during the next millennium, at least as a socio-economic phenomenon at the national and international levels. We have spent the last century converting crude oil into people, and when the crude oil is gone, then so will be the people and all those conveniences that rely on petroleum or other fossil fuels for their existence. Good examples of such conveniences include automobiles, motorcycles, airplanes, ships, tractors and other farm implements, warplanes, tanks, helicopters, and Humvees, many if not most electrical power generating plants, lawnmowers, gas, coal, and oil furnaces, gas stoves, most public transportation, and all manufactured goods whose production depends on fossil fuels either for energy or as chemical feedstock. The United States already is in a state of serious competition for fossil fuels, our main competitors being India, China, and Russia. Our nation is currently spending at least $200 million a day in a war that most reasonable people around the world believe is actually a war to control the global petroleum supply, or at least to prevent others from controlling it. So all the evidence indicates that we are now approaching a condition in which an exponentially increasing population has nearly used up its supply of a fixed resource. By *nearly* I mean within a few hundred years, again, but a blink in evolutionary time.

So the world of 4010 likely will be more familiar to the people of the first century than to people of the twenty-first century. We will use horses for transportation and our numbers will have diminished to whatever levels can be supported by agriculture without pesticides or artificial fertilizers, both of which are heavily dependent on fossil fuel supplies. When we fight wars, they will be with armies that walk or ride on horses and in wooden chariots instead of tanks, and do not fly in helicopters or jet planes. We are likely to have explosives, which the people of Roman times did not have, but the kinds and amounts are probably a matter of debate. We will fight mainly over water supplies, thus most wars are likely to be somewhat localized, a good example being the non-shooting, legal, war over the Republican River being conducted by the states of Kansas and Nebraska. Oceans will recover from their current over-fished condition, and we will probably start whaling again, once the technology for building wooden ships is rediscovered, a development that depends on reestablishment of adequate forests.

However, and this is a relatively important "however," we will be in this socio-economic-ecological state with our current knowledge of mathematics, art, music, and literature. It is entirely possible that the two- or three-hundred-year period from the global collapse of civilization and massive death to the readjustment of humans to Earth-imposed limits will be one of the most miserable times in all of human history. And it is equally possible that the following thousand years will be one of the richest, culturally speaking, in all human history, mainly because our capacity for destruction will have been so drastically reduced and we will have retained our knowledge of how to make art, music, and literature. Visitors from outer space, 20,000 years from now, might well discover magnificent cave art, equal in power to that of Lascaux, but produced some time during the Fourth Millennium.

There is little evidence from either the historical record or published psychological research to support a prediction that we will have "learned our lesson" about violence and environment destruction, thus purposefully achieving a harmonious relationship with our planet. Like today, many individuals will understand the need to live in such a way, but at the population level we are still going to be governed by our human genes, most of which we inherited from our nonhuman ancestor primates. These genes, and the behaviors they drive us into, are described well in E. O. Wilson's classic book *On Human Nature*, as well as a number of more recent works. Because of our genetic makeup, Wilson claims, human males will always live in dominance hierarchies populated by other males, and human females will always form mutually supportive groups capable of working together to solve problems. Our best prediction, therefore, is that two millennia hence, most if not all of us will resemble Ndani people of the New Guinea highlands more than the Silicon Valley entrepreneurs and *People* magazine cover story subjects.

Should we worry about this transition? Probably not, because there is not much we can do about it. Even if I said yes, we *should* worry a great deal about the changes coming for humanity in the next two thousand years nobody would listen to the advice. We worry about ourselves, our next meal, our children, and if we have some and they are cute and readily accessible, our grandchildren. We don't worry much about our neighbors down the street, nor about our neighbors' great-grandchildren-to-be, even when the neighbors are good friends. Instead, our worries are about what E. O. Wilson probably would predict, based on his understanding of primate genetic heritage. We focus our emotional energies on immediate needs and resources, factors that threaten our small extended family troop, and various real, imagined, or metaphorical bears at the cave door.

Just for the sake of discussion, instead of trying to think two millennia ahead of today, let us envision just the next five hundred years and perhaps do another thought experiment, again by assuming that natural processes we already know about will still be operational, that fossil fuel supplies will be exhausted within the first one or two hundred years of this half-millennium, and that fresh water supplies will also become limiting (as they are close to becoming at the present time). On the technical side, to our credit, we have nuclear energy as a possible substitute for much of the fossil fuel now consumed. Because nuclear energy has the capacity to actually replace so much of the fossil fuel use, our biggest choice, as a species, is whether that nuclear energy gets used for peaceful purposes—heating and lighting homes and schools, supplying electricity for trains and streetcars, sustaining communications networks, etc.—or military one—as weapons of mass destruction both manufactured and used. Thus the question becomes: are we going to use our brains and our highest, most noble character traits, exercising, in the process, unheralded rationality? Or are we going to fight?

If we decide, as a species, to use nuclear weapons against one another, then the question becomes whether such use is relatively limited or catastrophic. If it is catastrophic, then there is no point to discussing how humans will be living in the future. If nuclear wars are limited, then the resulting elimination of infrastructure, coupled with water and alternative fuel shortages (or absences!), much of humanity will be living in urban jungles characterized by violence and low-level conventional warfare. Baghdad in 2007 is a model for such a set of conditions. In the opening years of the Third Millennium, in order to understand what happens to humans when deprived of fuel, water, services, infrastructure, and tolerance, one only needs to read the morning paper or watch Fox News. This kind of degeneration should not be particularly startling; it has happened numerous times throughout history and currently happens fairly frequently (several African nations over the past half century).

Are the conditions described above conducive to organic evolution of humans over the next two thousand years? The answer is probably, if not emphatically "yes," especially given the fact that our species is evolving quite rapidly already. A general rule in population genetics is that the larger the population, the greater the genetic diversity within that population. The human population is now at least seven billion and growing rapidly, mostly in what we North Americans like to call "the developing world," whereas birthrates in the "developed world," meaning the United States and Europe, are stable or declining. Data to support this contention are available from a variety of web sites and in all freshman biology texts. Any reasonable scientist would conclude that yes, indeed, all the conditions are correct for very rapid evolution of *Homo sapiens*. That same biologist also would predict that the next species of human is likely to be darker, on the average, than the present one, and will be smaller and smarter in the same way that certain so-called primitive tribes are smart. In other words, the environment will dictate survival much more than we believe it does today, and those individuals who are mentally adept at picking up survival skills will produce the most offspring.

What are those skills likely to be? Again, the question is fairly easy to answer because we have so many good examples from the past century. These people will be highly resourceful, capable of forming small group alliances when necessary, and the bacterial flora of their digestive systems will be quite different from ours because of the mixture of foods they will be forced to eat. Those foods will be about anything that contains protein, and in the post-petroleum world the most readily available source of protein will be rats, cockroaches and other insects, chickens, pigeons, cattle, horses, dogs, and cats. For those living near the coasts, molluscs will be a major part of the diet, just as they were millennia in the past and still are for a large number of people in places like Baja California. The potential food species are generalists that seem to survive quite well under stressful conditions, and aside from the cats, are reasonably omnivorous. Vegetable components of the future humans' diet will be about anything that grows and is not poisonous. Finally, the population density of Fifth Millennium people will be much lower than at present, and large cities, if they exist, will be quite isolated from one another physically but probably not in terms of communication.

If there are large animals present two millennia hence, those are most likely to be horses, camels, or similar types of livestock, depending on the region. People will keep animals that serve multiple functions: as food, transportation, and labor. Coastal regions are likely to flourish because the capacity for destruction of marine life will be so drastically reduced. Thus whaling is very likely to make a comeback. This comeback will depend on forests, as mentioned above, to provide wood for ships, and on the ability of the oceans to support a food chain leading up to very large mammals. That ability in turn depends in large part on radiation, algae, and pelagic crustaceans. Provided we have not completely destroyed the ozone layer to the point of bathing the planet in ultraviolet rays, then oceanic algal populations are likely to flourish, which means that the remainder of the food chain is likely to flourish, too. So among the most fortunate and stable populations of the Fifth Millennium will be Eskimos, assuming they retain their ancestral knowledge of how to build kayaks and other whaling craft from available materials. The whaling industry in more temperate climes could easily rebound to what it was in the 18th and 19th centuries in the United States, but the industry is likely to experience cycles resulting from unregulated harvest. This time around, the meat will be consumed as well as the oil.

Will there be wars? Most certainly there will be wars, although it's a little difficult to predict what the weapons are likely to be, beyond those that were present prior to the discovery of petroleum. So as a minimum, we should expect warfare similar to that of the Romans. But there is one human trait that we should not ignore in this analysis of the future, and that is our ability to retain knowledge gained over the past. Humans of the Fifth Millennium will be exceedingly cunning in warfare, and probably exceedingly cruel, too, as they have been for all of recorded history, insofar as we know. We can expect extremes of torture and mutilation, coupled with social insults that produce major emotional trauma at the individual as well as social levels. Good examples of this situation already exist. For example, beheading of captives, especially when done slowly and in a ritual way, is emotionally wrenching, and in the absence of the Internet, we might well expect creative solutions to the communication problem. Many such solutions come to mind, but I'm reluctant to mention them in case someone might take them to heart now instead of waiting another two thousand years. As for social trauma elicited by words and pictures, one need only remember the Islamic reaction to those Danish cartoons depicting The Prophet Muhammed in less-than-flattering situations. There is little reason to believe that such conflict can be resolved through political means, and there is every reason to believe that in the future, wars will continue unabated for decades, even becoming ritualized, as they did in Ndani societies of New Guinea.

The major question regarding humanity's future is whether we will retain our electronic communication skills beyond the Age of Fossil Fuels. In the absence of truly catastrophic nuclear Armageddon we should be able to retain much of our electronic communication technology. If we subtract fossil fuels from the communications industry as it now exists then we lose repair vehicles, much of the manufacturing capacity, and energy supply. The latter can be replaced easily by nuclear power, but manufacturing and maintenance components remain a major question mark. Natural disasters such as Hurricane Katrina show clearly that electronic communication is heavily dependent on physical infrastructure, which in turn is built and maintained, at present, mostly through consumption of raw materials and fossil fuel. If infrastructure cannot be maintained, then electronic communications cannot, either. So the nature of future communications may well be the biggest question facing humanity over the next two thousand years. If we lose the capacity to communicate electronically, then our future is reasonably predictable although not altogether pleasant (see above); if we retain it, then our future is very unpredictable. Having already addressed the former case, let's consider the more challenging case.

By assuming that we retain electronic communication capacities, we also are assuming that we somehow manage to manufacture, maintain, and distribute communication devices and maintain electronic networks. Given these assumptions, then, the question becomes: what kind of a human society might develop with rapid global communications but without rapid global travel? We have a wide spectrum of choices. At the positive end of this spectrum is an almost utopian world in which people share ideas, literature, images, and advice on living within available resources; indeed, with Twitter, Facebook, and other Internet tools we are approaching that condition now.

At the negative end is a world of extreme cunning in which our primitive traits are enhanced, strengthened, and manipulated as groups compete with one another. In the latter case, males will operate in dominance hierarchies characterized by skill at use of information, females will be quite subordinate and relegated to groups integrated and controlled by information, and wars will be fought slowly but with extreme imagination and innovation regarding the use of available weapons. This condition will put a premium on intelligence, attention span, discipline, and creativity, something that is generally lacking among a large section of today's male population, at least in the United States. Thus we can anticipate a warrior class, a labor class, and an oligarchy of really smart and cunning males.

Given the record of *Homo sapiens* on Earth to date, I suspect that the utopian alternative is little more than wishful thinking and that war will be the norm, as it generally has been for much if not all of recorded history. Even today, in this grand experiment we call the United States of America our circumstances and official actions are beginning to resemble those spelled out in George Orwell's *1984*. The world is divided roughly into three main economic, religious, and social units: Asia, the Islamic Middle East, and Europe–Western Hemisphere. In the U.S. we have the Office of Homeland Security, the Patriot Act, video monitors in places ranging from busy intersections to convenience stores, and a hyperactive religious community with clear beliefs regarding Armageddon,

Rapture, and the imminent return of Jesus. We also have a diverse set of electronic gadgets that take information and send it around to all kinds of places at the speed of light: IP address checkers, Radio Frequency Identification Tags in credit cards, clothing, and pets, as well as similar identification chips embedded beneath our skin (if we want one), caller ID, spyware that reports your browsing habits, and online shopping sites that record your purchases and start recommending similar items. Were he living in Omaha today, Winston Smith, Orwell's Ministry of Truth bureaucrat, would see a lot of familiar circumstances.

Humans may be quite different from other animals in the extent to which we are self-aware, thus cognizant of our past and curious about our future, but we also require food, water, and shelter. We are no different from all other organisms in this respect. Water may exist as a fluid, solid, or gas, but it's always H_2O. Our food comes many various forms, but it's ultimately derived from plants, fungi, animals, and microbes—that is, non-human organisms, the ones with which we share the planet. In terms of potential food resources for the future, there is one prediction that is absolutely accurate: we are living in an age of mass extinction, and we are the cause.

Destruction of tropical forests alone validates this prediction because scientists estimate that about seventy percent of all genetic information present on Earth resides in these forests. That genetic information comes primarily in the form of microbes, plants, and animals, especially insects. Although most of these species probably are inedible, many also may play important roles in pollination and seed dispersal, processes that are essential for the health of terrestrial ecosystems. We are now obliterating this wealth of biological resources at a frantic pace, producing not only agricultural products, at least in the short term, but mass extinction, social upheaval, political conflict, and additional cycles of environmental destruction and its consequences. Humans are simply killing off the world's biota faster, and more effectively, than it has been destroyed by natural causes at any time in Earth's history.

The fossil record tells us a great deal about mass extinctions because it provides evidence that several have occurred over the past half-billion years and allows us to track their long-term consequences. At the end of the Permian Period, approximately 230 million years ago, at least 90% of all known genera disappeared. Today's coal deposits were laid down prior to this time, during the Carboniferous Period, and in some places, coal contains an abundance of ancient plant fossils. That record also shows that large extinctions occurred during the Carboniferous. And, of course, the disappearance of North American megafauna (mammoths, ground sloths, etc.) was a much more recent event that some have attributed to human activity, at least in part.

The net effect of mass extinctions is substantial loss of biological diversity, followed by evolutionary diversification from the remaining genetic stock. Animal life today, for example, is far less diverse, in terms of basic body architecture, than it was 500 million years ago. Stephen J. Gould documents this reduction of diversity in his book *Wonderful Life: The Burgess Shale and the Nature of History*, showing us what Earth has lost in terms of exotic creatures. Such loss of genetic diversity is called a genetic bottleneck. Cheetahs and pandas are well-known cases that illustrate the idea. *Homo sapiens*, with its enormous capacity for environmental destruction, may well be the champion of all evolutionary forces, generating bottlenecks more rapidly than, and perhaps surpassing, those produced by continental drift, climate change, and volcanic catastrophe over the past billion years. The fossil record also shows that widespread extinction is followed by subsequent diversification from a much-reduced supply of genes; Earth loses themes, but gets many variations on the ones remaining.

Two thousand years equals about a hundred human reproductive cycles, certainly enough time for our species to become noticeably smaller and darker, especially if confronted with no petroleum, rapidly increasing global temperature, and limited freshwater supplies. If we extend our thought experiment to millions rather than thousands of years and ask what the descendents of *Homo sapiens* will be like in five million years, the potential answers become very interesting indeed. Much of this interest stems from the fact that we already have a model for primate evolution over a similar period in the past: divergence of chimpanzees from early species of genus *Homo*. We also have a model for major changes in large animals over extended periods: the evolution of dinosaurs into modern birds. For a truly imaginative scientist with these models, it's not too difficult to conjure up an extremely intelligent and cunning little brown primate, perhaps the size of a squirrel, eating rodents and insects, cultivating certain plants, protecting itself with deadly natural poisons on hair-thin darts, sitting around tiny fires singing magically beautiful quiet songs and telling novels to adolescent children the size of today's mice.

◆　　◆　　◆

In the last four chapters I have tried to address questions that as a scientist I believe are of paramount importance to our nation. This belief is based on what I've learned about our interactions with the natural world during the past half century, most of it spent on the prairies of North America, a continent on the single planet known to support life of any kind. All organisms have one-sided relationships with this planet; they take space, energy, raw building materials, and water from it, and only because most organisms are wild do they ever return these items. So the taking is built into life, but the giving is by default and happenstance. As long as there is plenty of space, energy, raw materials, and water, taking is of little consequence. In fact, such taking produces diversity through evolution, an intrinsically interesting phenomenon, and one that would very likely be quite interesting to intelligent aliens from a galaxy far, far away. On a large scale, prior to the appearance of humans, taking was generally matched by return: when a large tree, or a big dinosaur, died, it became space, energy, and raw materials for other organisms.

Humans interpret this natural taking and giving as cyclic, putting diagrams into biology textbooks and labeling them "The Carbon Cycle," "The Nitrogen Cycle," "The Water Cycle," etc. Humans disrupt these cycles by putting carbon and nitrogen into forms such as plastics and other molecules that cannot be readily digested by bacteria and fungi, thus cannot be returned. We also have an enormous capacity for destruction, equal, in my view, to our capacity for intellectual endeavor. A lifetime's educational experiences should, ideally, reveal both the warning of destruction and the wonder of art, science, music, and literature. The warning and the wonder are not unlike the bleached boards and deep shadows on Aunt Ethel's farm. They are the alternate sides of reality that you see through experience: the subtle but elusive complexity of a flat horizon over upright grass, a native's rich visual world against the visitor shading his eyes in the glare, and timeless memories bound so tightly to the calling of an insect.

In *Pieces of the Plains* I have tried to lead you on a roundabout journey from recent past to a relatively distant future, a journey in which I've described where and how a person's awareness of the natural world arises, how this awareness is enhanced and developed over an individual lifetime, how it is enriched so strongly by family involvement in the arts, and finally how it forces one to think about centuries ahead. If there is a central theme to this book, it's that of education in the broadest sense, a constant learning derived from exploration of things and places like cottonwood bark and barbed wire on Ethel Campbell's farm, a single drop of filthy water swarming with life, a pasture with a horse, a faculty meeting rife with academic and gender politics, a stroll through an art museum, coffee with a group of students, and thought experiments involving cell phones and first-century Israelites.

Such education is a product of good fortune. In our conversations, Karen and I often remind ourselves of this luck: born in a nation where we can criticize government without getting arrested, assemble with our friends, attend whatever church we choose, flip through a hundred television stations, and read publications that explore in depth the successes and failures of those in positions of power. To that good fortune, add choices made mainly out of self-interest: to ask a coed to dance at a dorm social in 1958, to answer a job advertisement posted by the University of Nebraska, to become a college professor, and, in Karen's case, to volunteer at what was then named The Sheldon Memorial Art Gallery.

10 WHAT WILL HUMAN LIFE BE LIKE IN A COUPLE OF THOUSAND YEARS?

Each choice opened some doors but locked others permanently. Children, when they arrived, were decisions made for us—Cynthia Anne, unnamed for five days in a Norman, Oklahoma, hospital, while Karen held her and we wracked our brains for just the right one for this little individual who was quite different than we'd imagined her to be; Jenifer Lynn, recipient of that name I'd picked for Cindy, for whom it seemed totally wrong, but then seemed totally right for the tiny blond second child; and John III, whose name had been long decided, by Karen, unless he'd been a girl. That those three children are now grown, independent, well-educated, professionals is something we also marvel at during our evening glass of wine, before Karen picks up the Lincoln *Journal Star*'s daily crossword puzzle and I plunge into *The New Yorker*.

Pieces of the Plains can thus be considered a sort of memoir, but one in which experience is the main character, instead of the writer. Our nation—the United States of America—also is a prime character, for all the reasons mentioned in the above paragraphs—freedom of speech, of assembly, of religion (or *from* religion, if one so chooses), of the press, and freedom to succeed or fail on one's own merits if given equal opportunity. Those privileged freedoms are the heart of a magnificent nation; they also are the breeding ground for ideas that seem logical at the time they are expressed but end up leading us into actions we regret, especially at the national level, actions that often have their greatest impacts on individual lives. In this sense we are all participants in history, regardless of whether our names end up in textbooks.

This book is thus my own personal lesson—simply one more case study—in how the past informs one's thoughts about a future. The heart of America is filled with such studies, one for every person who has lived within our national boundaries. My hope is that two thousand years from now there will still be those same freedoms and constitutional guarantees as birthrights, prairies upon which a young person can venture, and a friend who invites the kid to lunch, orders a Stoli martini, and offers to help him tell his stories about the past, the present, and the future.

Acknowledgments, Notes, and Sources

I would like to give sincere thanks to Rhonda and Jim Seacrest for suggesting and supporting this book project. As indicated in the Foreword, not many people ever get the opportunity to write, and publish, without being subjected to market-driven editorial decisions, so *Pieces of the Plains* is indeed a remarkable gift—to me—and a privilege that is hard to describe completely. I also need to thank my wife Karen, first for permission to actually use material from our visit to Woodward, Oklahoma, and from those months of her mother's terminal illness, and second for careful reading and editing of much the manuscript. Karen regularly saves me from serious embarrassment and this book is no exception, although there's no guarantee I didn't change something back after she'd corrected it. Finally, thanks to Shay Hampton, an undergraduate honors researcher in my lab, who agreed to an interview about her University of Nebraska–Lincoln experiences; material from that interview is included in the chapter entitled "The Firm."

Other readers who looked at this manuscript include Paige Ahart, a UNL sophomore. I sent out an e-mail to several undergraduates from Biology 101, fall, 2008, asking whether they were interested in some office work, and as a result, Paige volunteered to be a serious reader, with a focus on content, sequence, and usage; her comments were exceptionally valuable. Alaine Knipes and Gabe Langford, both doctoral students in my lab at the time of writing, Matt Bolek a former graduate student, and Ben Vogt, a recent English PhD who was a student in a class I once taught entitled "Writing About Nature," all saw, and made comments on, at least some of the manuscript at various stages of completion. David Lechner, University of Nebraska Vice President for Business and

182

Finance (and golfing buddy), and Carmen Mauer, Associate General Counsel, both screened chapter 6, "The Firm," for compliance with institutional policies. I also need to acknowledge Jim McKee of J & L Lee Company for his expertise and advice relative to the book's production, and Sheri Ericksen, the designer, who contributed technical advice.

The Firm, a.k.a. UNL, has provided me with a truly wonderful professional life that turned out to be intellectually, culturally, socially, and politically rich beyond my imagination when I joined the faculty in 1966. I knew when I started this job that there would be a long parade of students through my classes and laboratory; what I didn't realize was that this parade would be the key to a successful career. So to every parent who has sent a child to UNL, I say thanks for the pleasure and privilege of associating with these bright and talented young people.

Each chapter has a small drawing related to one of the important artifacts, ideas, or sources used in the writing. All these illustrations are originals and their subjects are indicated below.

1. Ethel

The cicada drawing was made at UNL's Cedar Point Biological Station in western Nebraska, and was a birthday gift to Karen. Details of the Campbell clan come from Karen's family records, some of which were supplied by Dolores White of Norman, Oklahoma (Karen's sister). John Spence is a Lincoln artist and still shows his work in local galleries. Statistical information about farming comes from world almanacs (*The World Almanac® and Book of Facts*). I own editions from 1959 to 1999 and consult others regularly in the library. Information about Buffalo Commons comes from Internet sources.

Books:
> Famighetti, R. (Editorial Director) 1999. *The World Almanac® and Book of Facts*. Mahwah, NJ: World Almanac Books, Primedia Reference Inc. 1008p.
> Matthiessen, P. 1975. *Far Tortuga*. New York: Random House, Inc. 407p. (epigraph)

Internet sources:
> en.wikipedia.org/wiki/Vincent_van_Gogh
> www.buffalocommons.org/

www.hcn.org/issues/194/10194
www.landinstitute.org/vnews/display.v/ART/2004/08/04/
   41223655825ae
www.longhaulpro.org/pages/series/heartland.html
www.plainsfolk.com/buffalocommons/

2. Genevieve

The illustration for this chapter is made from scans of the recipe cards given to Karen by her stepmother Genevieve Oneth of El Reno, Oklahoma. Genevieve evidently copied the recipe down from a radio broadcast in the 1950s. Since the chapter was written, some of the people mentioned have moved and some of their activities have changed, but for a variety of reasons I decided to leave the narrative unchanged.

Books:

   Kaufman, K. 1935. *Level Land: A Book of Western Verse*. Dallas, TX: The Kaleidograph Press. 85p. (epigraph)

Internet sources:

   Information about Tinker Air Force Base comes from their official web site and associated links. www.tinker.af.mil/

3. Red Dirt

The geologist's pick in the drawing was my grandfather Frank's, retrieved from his house when he died and my Aunt Helen moved, from that house, into another one in Oklahoma City. A copy of Uranium in Oklahoma was found in Helen's house after she died. Population information comes from The World Almanac® and Book of Facts.

Books:

   Jordan, L. 1957. *Subsurface Stratigraphic Names of Oklahoma*. Norman, OK: Oklahoma Geological Survey. 220p. (epigraph)

4. Through a Lens

The pen and ink drawing was done from the toy microscope discussed in the chapter and a jar used in my UNL lab to make an infusion culture for teaching purposes. The jar has actually had weeds, water, and microorganisms growing in it and has been returned to the lab.

Books:

   Dobell, C. 1932. *Antony van Leewenhoek and His Little Animals*. New York: Harcourt, Brace and Company. 435p. (epigraph)

Internet sources:
www.talkorigins.org/faqs/homs/specimen.html
www.ucmp.berkeley.edu/chromista/browns/phaeofr.html

5. The Horse (and Introduction to The Horse)

The horse's foot was drawn from my photograph of "Apache," courtesy of Scott Capps, Pioneer Stables, Lincoln, NE; the kangaroo rat was drawn using anatomical information from a variety of sources. "The Horse," but not the "Introduction," is an excerpt from *The Ginkgo: An Intellectual and Visionary Coming-of-Age.*

Books:
Janovy, J. Jr. 2009. *The Ginkgo: An Intellectual and Visionary Coming-of-Age.* Lincoln, NE: The Protistan Press. 334p. (Amazon and Kindle)

Nye, W. S. 1962. *Bad Medicine & Good: Tales of the Kiowas.* Norman, OK: University of Oklahoma Press. 291p. (epigraph)

6. The Firm

The drawing is of UNL's Memorial Stadium as seen from my laboratory window. The epigraph quote from George Ade was obtained from William Zinsser's On Writing Well (30th Anniversary Edition, paperback); Russo's bibliography of Ade did not contain a fable with that name.

Books:
Bartlett, J. 1980. Familiar Quotations: A collection of Passages, Phrases and Proverbs Traced to Their Sources in Ancient and Modern Literature. 15th Ed., (E. M. Beck, Ed.) Boston, MA: Little, Brown and Company. 1540p. (epigraph)

Russo, D. R. 1947. *A bibliography of George Ade 1866-1944.* Indianapolis, IN: Indiana Historical Society. 314p.

Zinsser, W. 2006. *On Writing Well: The Classic Guide to Writing Nonfiction* (30th Anniversary Edition). New York: HarperCollins Publishers. 321p. (epigraph)

Journals:
Gardiner, J. R. 2009. At liberty to divulge: one student's perspective from inside Jerry Falwell's university. *American Scholar,* 78:131-133. (epigraph)

Internet sources:
en.wikipedia.org/wiki/Camera_lucida
www.amanet.org/books/catalog/0814472990_Timeline.htm
www.cdc.gov/ncidod/eid/vol8no4/01-0273.htm
www.ncbi.nlm.nih.gov/pubmed/11719488

7. What is Science?

The illustration is a PowerPoint figure I made for an undergraduate honors researcher, Kristin Brotan, and posted on our lab door to remind her of the labor involved in science. Kristin did a spectacular undergraduate thesis.

Books:

Kuhn, T. S. 1996. *The Structure of Scientific Revolutions*, 3rd Ed. Chicago: University of Chicago Press. 212p.

Sobel, D. 1999. *Galileo's Daughter: A Historical Memoir of Science, Faith, and Love*. New York: Walker Publishing Company, Inc. 420p.

Wilson, E. O. 1998. *Concilience: The Unity of Knowledge*. New York: Alfred A. Knopf. 332p. (epigraph)

Journals:

Fischetti, M. 2001. Drowning New Orleans. *Scientific American*, 285:76-85.

Internet sources:

en.wikipedia.org/wiki/Effects_of_Hurricane_Katrina_on_New_Orleans

www.usa.gov/Citizen/Topics/PublicSafety/Hurricane_Katrina_Recovery.shtml

8. Why are Politicians so Scientifically Illiterate?

The drawing is based on a sketch from a faculty meeting; I've used the idea in numerous presentations to various audiences.

Books:

McPhee, J. 1989. *The Control of Nature*. New York: Farrar, Straus and Giroux, 272 p.

Tuchman, B. W. 1970. *Stilwell and the American Experience in China, 1911-1945*. New York: The Macmillan Company, 621p. (epigraph)

Journals:

Schawlow, A. L., and C, H. Townes. 1958. Infrared and Optical Masers. *Physical Review*, 112:1940-1949.

Internet sources:

en.wikipedia.org/wiki/No_Child_Left_Behind_Act

www.advocatesforyouth.org/publications/stateevaluations/index.htm – abstinence only info

www.bell-labs.com/history/laser/

www.ed.gov/policy/elsec/leg/esea02/index.html

www.gallup-international.com

www.iraqupdates.com/p_articles.php/article/54343
en.wikipedia.org/wiki/Iraq_War

9. What is a Human Being?

The drawing is of our son, John III, in the early 1970s, playing in a rain puddle outside my parents' former house on Colony Lane in Oklahoma City. That house has since burned under mysterious circumstances. Writing about the Musée du Quai Branly comes directly from a visit there, where my first reaction was "What was going through their minds when they made that?"

Books:

Dawkins, R. 1976. *The Selfish Gene.* New York: The Oxford University Press, 224p.

Farb, P. 1968. *Man's rise to civilization as shown by the Indians of North America from primeval times to the coming of the industrial state.* New York: Dutton 332p. (epigraph)

Thomas, L. 1974. *Lives of a Cell: Notes of a Biology Watcher.* New York: The Viking Press. 153p.

Internet sources:

www.nationalcowboymuseum.org/
www.quaibranly.fr/en/
www.tate.org.uk/modern/

10. What will Human Life be Like in a Couple of Thousand Years?

The drawing is a self-portrait based on a photograph posed for the purpose of making the drawing; the hatchet was one bought by my father, probably in the early 1950s; the bottle is one from my lab. The hatchet represents global deforestation; the bottle represents the consequent loss of genetic diversity (bottleneck); the label, SAPIENS, means "wise," as in *Homo sapiens* (wise man), although collectively we're acting anything but wise; and, the watch reads five minutes before midnight.

Books:

Diamond, J. 2005. *Collapse: How Societies Choose to Fail or Succeed.* New York: Viking Press. 575p.

Drake, F., and D. Sobel. 1992. *Is Anyone Out There?: The Scientific Search for Extraterrestrial Intelligence.* New York, N.Y.: Delacorte Press, 272p. (epigraph)

Gould, S. J. 1989. *Wonderful life : the Burgess Shale and the nature of history*. New York: W. W. Norton and Company, 347p.

Orwell, G. 1949. *Nineteen Eighty-Four*. London: Secker and Warburg Publishers. 326p.

Wilson, E. O. 1978. *On Human Nature*. Cambridge: Harvard University Press. 260p.

Internet Sources:

earthobservatory.nasa.gov/Features/Deforestation/

en.wikipedia.org/wiki/Dani_people

en.wikipedia.org/wiki/List_of_countries_and_territories_by_fertility_rate

en.wikipedia.org/wiki/Nostradamus

news.cnet.com/Human-chips-more-than-skin-deep/2009-1008_3-5318076.html

news.mongabay.com/2008/0515-hance_myers.html

en.wikipedia.org/wiki/The_Flintstones

en.wikipedia.org/wiki/The_Jetsons

www.ucsusa.org/global_warming/science_and_impacts/impacts/tropical-deforestation-and.html